Thriving
after
Divorce

Thriving
after
Divorce

Transforming your life when a relationship ends

Tonja Evetts Weimer

ATRIA PAPERBACK
New York London Toronto Sydney

BEYOND WORDS
Hillsboro, Oregon

ATRIA PAPERBACK

A Division of Simon & Schuster, Inc.
1230 Avenue of the Americas
New York, NY 10020

BEYOND WORDS

20827 N.W. Cornell Road, Suite 500
Hillsboro, Oregon 97124-9808
503-531-8700 / 503-531-8773 fax
www.beyondword.com

Copyright © 2010 by Tonja Evetts Weimer

Managing editor: Lindsay S. Brown
Editor: Julie Steigerwaldt
Copyeditor: Meadowlark Publishing Services
Proofreader: Jade Chan
Design: Devon Smith
Composition: William H. Brunson Typography Services

First Atria Paperback/Beyond Words trade paperback edition March 2010

ATRIA PAPERBACK and colophon are trademarks of Simon & Schuster, Inc.
Beyond Words Publishing is a division of Simon & Schuster, Inc.

For more information about special discounts for bulk purchases, please contact Simon & Schuster Special Sales at 1-866-506-1949 or business@simonandschuster.com.

The Simon & Schuster Speakers Bureau can bring authors to your live event. For more information or to book an event, contact the Simon & Schuster Speakers Bureau at 1-866-248-3049 or visit our website at www.simonspeakers.com.

Manufactured in the United States of America

10 9 8 7 6 5 4 3 2 1

Library of Congress Cataloging-in-Publication Data

Weimer, Tonja Evetts.
    Thriving after divorce : transforming your life when a relationship ends / Tonja Evetts Weimer.
        p. cm.
    1. Divorce. 2. Divorce—Psychological aspects. 3. Divorced people—Life skills guides. 4. Self-actualization (Psychology). I. Title.

HQ814.W444 2010
306.89—dc22

                                                                    2009043588

ISBN: 978-1-58270-248-3
ISBN: 978-1-4391-6480-8 (ebook)

The corporate mission of Beyond Words Publishing, Inc.: *Inspire to Integrity*

To Vik, my biggest fan

Contents

Acknowledgments

If you believe in miracles, then you will understand this page of gratitude. Sometimes in life, the cosmic forces converge to support a project you want to bring to others. With *Thriving After Divorce*, the heavens opened and brought energies together that made this book possible.

I am deeply grateful to Cynthia Black for her vision, commitment, and continuing desire to be a catalyst in providing the world with enlightenment. Lindsay Brown and the staff at Beyond Words/Simon & Schuster gave the help and encouragement that kept the book alive and moving. Julie Steigerwaldt was a dream of an editor with her insight, talent, and patience. Thanks to Danielle Marshall and Whitney Quon for their practical, as well as motivational support. And if it weren't for my agent, Susan Crawford, we wouldn't be reading this page, not to mention the book, right now.

It means everything when you have someone like my husband, Vik Pearce, to be Mr. Head Cheerleader and keep the enthusiasm aloft, even when I was flagging. I thank Sue Inman for being a great teacher, Amy Richmond for her superior counsel, and the Tuesday night writing class for providing the space for me to use my creative muscles.

Acknowledgments

I appreciate the generosity of spirit in the letters from the readers of my newspaper column, *Savvy Dating*. I treasure my clients who gave me the inspiration to persevere, just as they did with their own personal challenges. I am also indebted to my children, family members, and friends who reminded me, over and over, that I was surrounded by their love and unshakable belief in my mission.

For all of this and more, I am grateful.

Introduction

I wish I'd had a book like this when I was going through a divorce. No one suggested that there was a way to take the high road and leave all the parties involved still standing. That's why I wanted and needed to write *Thriving After Divorce*—a spiritual guide that will help you discover how to use your divorce or breakup as an inspiration for positive change. It will challenge you to look within to find your best self. Your community of friends, family, children, and even business associates are all affected when your relationship dissolves. Whether you are going through a divorce or a breakup, ending a partnership with fairness, kindness, and consideration to those around you will serve you for the rest of your life.

Divorces and breakups are notoriously negative processes, complete with blame, fault, and suffering. So much is needlessly lost because the romantic alliance has ended. Many people have a personal history with their ex that goes back as far as high school or even childhood. Relationships with friends, family, and in-laws become blurred in the emotional turmoil. And the shared history becomes distorted.

As this book will show you, relationships don't need to end this way. Using the new model for divorce that I have developed, you will learn how to reach for a higher ground to forge a different kind of separation. The romance may end, but many other levels of partnership can still exist. When you understand and set strong boundaries, you will find that you can practice civility and even compassion, which makes the transition so much smoother. Separation can truly be a transformative process that leaves you in a stronger, healthier, more fulfilling place than the one you were in when you started.

Everyone who has been through a breakup or divorce has a story to tell. Here is mine:

At the age of thirty-seven, I was alone in a large new city with three small children. I had given up my exciting career as a consultant to school systems and creator of educational materials to raise the kids. I had no money or job. My family and friends were thousands of miles away. I had cut myself off from all support systems. Having cosigned many loans, I had large amounts of debt on my shoulders. I had reached this place because I kept waiting for my husband to take care of me. Hanging on and hoping things would get better in the marriage only made things worse. He left. I was overwhelmed; I could barely drag myself through the day.

If I had been a coach then, as I am now, I would have told the *old* me, Be still. Get quiet and don't waste your energy thinking "My life is over." Life as you knew it may be over, but your new life is just beginning. Listen to your spiritual self, which knows how to do what is right. When you tap that source, you will discover the voice that nurtures you, accepts you, and prepares you for the next steps on your path.

Finally, I stepped up to learning what my life's choices were trying to teach me. Drop by drop I began to fill my empty cup. I found seminars, classes, conferences, support groups, spiritual retreats, and books for self-growth. I searched for people to talk to, found inspiring teachers, and met survivors who had made their lives immeasurably better, no matter what their odds. Along the way, I learned a valuable lesson: you can change the quality of your life. This book will give you the tools to succeed and the support systems necessary for positive change. You can do better, you can be better, and you can have the life you've always wanted.

Once I learned how to do this for myself, I wanted to help other people find their way. I went back to school and became a life coach and a singles' relationship coach. My years of experience in training school systems and businesses to find and use their creative powers to achieve results are now melded with my coaching skills. This professional background, combined with living through hard times and divorce as well as my personal quest for a deeper, more spiritual life, has inspired the birth of *Thriving After Divorce*.

Over the years, I've developed processes that have helped my clients, both men and women, move through their own transformative experiences of divorce. Now you, too, can be part of a *different* relationship with your ex, your past, and yourself. Consider *Thriving After Divorce* to be a friend and personal guide to your exciting transformation.

With many blessings,
Tonja
March 16, 2010

1
The TAO of Divorce

The dissolution of your marriage or relationship brings you an enormous opportunity. By embracing this time of change, and the significant alterations to your life that it requires, you are letting go of what has come to an end and allowing the mystery of your future to unfold.

Some change is not welcome, but it happens nonetheless. Resisting the inevitable takes enormous energy, and that kind of emotional expenditure doesn't feed your soul. The path to finding the magic in this time is to release your grip on what is no longer meant to be and flow into your new realms of possibility. There may be times when it doesn't feel like it, but you're actually on the threshold of stepping into the best parts of yourself as you forge a new friendship with your partner.

This is your moment in life to find an empowering way of thinking about your breakup. How do you do that? By discovering the TAO of Divorce.

The word *Tao* comes from an ancient Chinese philosophy meaning "the Way." It is based on the understanding that the only constant in the Universe is *change*. The Tao is manifested through cycles and transitions.

If the romance is over between you and your mate, you are now in a new cycle of your partnership and your life, and you are transitioning into something unknown. Transitions can be hard and full of uncertainty. But you can approach this change armed with fresh practices and ideas to guide you through the present and the future. The Tao will help you become fluid—more like water than ice.

I use the three letters *T, A,* and *O* as an acronym for a useful process that will allow the Way to work through you. The letters represent Take, Actions, and Outcome. The following diagram explains the TAO:

The TAO of Divorce

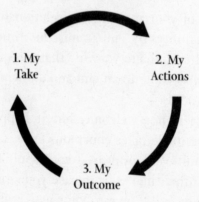

1. My Take

2. My Actions

3. My Outcome

What is a Take? It's the engine that drives your life. Your Take is how you see the world. It is a world seen through a lens shaped by everything you are and have ever experienced. Your gender, culture, family of origin, teachers, genetics, health, religion, country, successes, traumas, stories, and a million other pieces of information all form it. Your Take has absolutely *nothing* to do with reality, but it is your reality. It belongs solely to you. And as such, you have the power to shape it.

Every Take (your perception) leads to your Actions. Those Actions are what you do to express your Take, and they always lead to your Outcome (your results). That Outcome reaffirms your Take. This is a clear picture of how you can get stuck in a belief or perspective that does not serve you. It is only by *shifting* your Take that you will change your Actions, and, ultimately, your Outcome.

With divorce, your TAO becomes especially important when you are relating to your ex, your former in-laws, and your mutual friends. Obviously, a negative Take will lead to negative Actions, which will lead to an Outcome that is not conducive to resolving crucial issues. Also, a negative Take is not emotionally healthy for you—or for your children, family members, and even business associates.

This is not to say that you may not have some very real and valid reasons for holding a negative Take. Some breakups may be amicable, but many others are the result of affairs, abuse, or egregious loss of trust. Even for people who peaceably decide to split, the divorce process itself may bring out the worst in them. It can be a hurtful, messy, contentious, and stressful time. You are certainly entitled to feel your pain and acknowledge your suffering. But you likely picked up this book because you are ready to move on from the anguish to arrive at a higher place. Your thoughtfully constructed Take will get you there.

Here's an example of how a negative Take on your partner may play out:

- Your Take on your partner/ex: "He never listens to me! We can't communicate!"
- Your Actions: When you see him, you act resentful.
- Your Outcome: He is abrupt, angry, or cold.
- Your Take is reaffirmed by your Outcome. He doesn't listen to you. You accomplish nothing.

Now let's see what this would look like if you readjust your Take. Can you accept the fact that your partner is not a good listener?

3

Can you allow him to be the way he is and let it go? If the romance is over, can you stop being invested in wanting him to change to accommodate you?

After thinking about those questions, let's start with a new Take. For whatever reason, your partner is not a good listener, and you accept that fact. Can you think of something that is good about him? Everyone has *something*. Let's assume he used to be funny. When you relate to him in the future, hold the picture of his humor in your mind.

- Your new Take: He has a great sense of humor.
- Your new Actions: You are more relaxed, remembering his amusing side. You are not as edgy or resentful; you know who he is and you don't expect him to be different.
- Your new Outcome: You are better at discussing the important areas of your divorce, and your interaction is smoother.

Let's look at a common Take during or after divorce: "My ex is a jerk." If you hold this thought, you will probably treat your ex like a jerk, whether you are aware of it or not. The reaction you receive—your Outcome—can only be more negative behavior from your former partner. Instead, consider this thought: "My ex is a human being. All human beings deserve kindness, and I can and will try to be kind whenever we see or talk to each other."

When we hold a negative Take, we often look for validation for our perception. For instance, whatever it was that went "wrong" in your relationship, did you want to run to your friends and family and tell them about it? Did you feel like you needed understanding and agreement and for the people closest to you to be invested in your side of the story?

This was the case for me once my marriage was over. I was like Chicken Little; the sky was definitely falling, and I had to tell everyone. It seemed that the more people I had invested in my story, the more "right" I was.

I think of that analogy because once when I visited a classroom as a consultant, I heard a teacher telling a group of children the Chicken Little story. When an acorn fell on Chicken Little's head, he ran to tell all the barnyard animals that the sky was falling. He told Goosey-Loosey, Henny-Penny, Ducky-Lucky, and more. Gathering momentum, they all ran to tell the farmer.

At that point, the teacher asked the children, "What do you think that farmer thought when Chicken Little said, 'The sky is falling! The sky is falling!'?"

One little boy jumped out of his seat and yelled, "I'll bet that farmer thought, 'Holy sh**! A talking chicken!'"

That child's response certainly changed the trajectory of the story that day. It took a minute for the teacher to gather herself together. But the point for the rest of us is this: Chicken Little had a misconception. Not only did he have incorrect information but he was also basing his decisions and actions on what he perceived.

Both Chicken Little and I had to get a new perspective on what was happening in our lives. Convincing others that our story was true didn't make it truer. It just meant that we were good at getting others to buy into our perception. And until you shift that view, you can gather a lot of agreement from people that nothing is your "fault," life is hard, your ex is to blame, divorce is a tragedy, and more. None of these Takes will empower you. When you recognize that, it's time to redirect your energy toward forming a positive Take.

The TAO in Action

One of my clients is a lovely young woman whose life became more and more negative the longer she stayed in her marriage.

When Mary Ann came to me, she knew she needed to leave her husband to save herself, but she didn't know how she could do it without destroying her family.

Mary Ann had been married for ten years and had a six-year-old daughter. Earnest and smart, she was an entrepreneur who managed her family's construction business. She had started operating the business for her father when she graduated from college, and was now the key person who found clients for the company.

She told me that ever since getting married, she had felt a great deal of stress and depression. Her husband was reclusive and secretive, and when he did talk, he was verbally abusive. Mary Ann said she could no longer keep up the charade of marriage. She revealed that she and her husband had not had sex in more than two years. They went to couples' counseling, but after a few visits, he hated it and refused to go back. He thought Mary Ann needed therapy but he himself did not. He thought all their problems were in her imagination or were her fault.

Mary Ann felt trapped. She had put him in charge of all building projects and woven her husband's work life so tightly into her family's business that she didn't know how to extricate herself, and she felt the family business would be bankrupt in less than six months if she left her husband. Then they wouldn't be able to make their mortgage and car payments. She feared what the fallout of divorce would do to her child, to her parents, and to her own mental health. In her mind, if the marriage failed, everyone would fall.

Sympathizing with her situation, I asked, "Can we put the marriage on pause for a while? Visualize placing everything about it in a silver box tied with a ribbon, and put it up on a shelf for now. We can see it, we know it's there, and we'll address it later. Right now, let's take the focus off your husband and the marriage and focus on you. Tell me what you need."

She blinked away tears, was quiet for a full minute, and then said in a small voice, "I have no idea what I need. Right now, I'd settle for a little consideration."

"How much consideration do you give yourself?" I asked.

"I never think about myself," she said. "I'm so busy taking care of my daughter, waiting on my parents, who aren't well, keeping the books, finding clients for the business, volunteering at my child's school, and making enough money to take care of everyone that there is no time for me."

"It sounds like you make time for everyone else. What keeps you from making time for you?"

"I guess I think everyone else's needs are more important than mine."

I explained the concept of the TAO to Mary Ann. "Let's look at your TAO."

- Mary Ann's Take: Everyone else's needs come first.
- Mary Ann's Actions: Managing the business, dealing with her husband's outbursts, tending to her parents and child, and meeting payroll.
- Mary Ann's Outcome: Everyone's needs except hers get met. She feels empty, unappreciated, and stressed. Everyone in the family wants more, demands more, and expects more from her.
- Mary Ann's reaffirmation of her Take: Everyone's needs are more important than mine.

"Can you see the circular pattern you are caught in?" I asked.

Mary Ann listened and answered, "I think I need to look at things differently. I suppose I need a new Take."

"Yes," I agreed. "And I would like for you to spend the next week listening to your inside voice that says things to you all day, every day. Write every judgmental, accusing comment down. Some of them are so ingrained that you don't even know you are thinking them. We have thousands of thoughts a day, and most of them are negative. After you identify these internal Takes, see if you can reframe them into something positive.

"Let's start with changing 'Everyone else's needs are more important than mine' into something that states your importance.

"First of all, what are some of your daily needs that you don't pay attention to?"

"Well," Mary Ann said, "I get so busy that I forget to eat lunch. I never see my friends because I'm too busy and too unhappy. I used to work out every day and take a hike in the woods, but that was a long time ago. There are so many things I've dropped."

"Let's address your needs in your new Take."

Mary Ann said, "I like this Take: I deserve to meet my needs."

Mary Ann's Action steps for the next few weeks were to

1. Write down the negative phrases running through her mind that invalidate her.

2. Say her new affirming Take daily.

3. Spend half an hour a day attending to her needs.

The next time we got together, Mary Ann said she was doing a better job of staying out of confrontations with her husband, but her need to leave him was becoming increasingly urgent.

We looked for the defining moments in Mary Ann's life that had helped form her self-limiting Takes. She still wasn't ready to make the move toward divorce because she didn't want to let people down. That was a big issue for her.

"When did you let people down in the past?" I asked.

She told me that when she was young she was a gymnast, and her parents, coaches, and community were emotionally and financially invested in her qualifying for the Olympics. One week before the trials, she broke her ankle. She never forgot how she thought she had let everyone down. She said people still remembered this from twenty years ago and mentioned it when they saw her. Mary Ann interpreted their words to mean "We are so disappointed in *you*."

"What was your Take from that experience?" I asked.

"I guess that I'm a loser."

"Where's the evidence that you are a loser? Have you ever given yourself credit for what an amazing young girl you were? Did you ever let yourself feel talented and skilled and incredible? You might not have gotten to the Olympics, and yes, that is sad, but how about all those other ribbons and medals and awards you won? Looking back, do you think that little girl was a loser? Of course not.

"This is what we do to ourselves when we have had tough moments in our lives. We replay them in our minds, judging or condemning ourselves, and then live from the lie that we are not enough or we don't deserve anything.

"How would you change that Take, 'I am a loser,' today?"

I could see recognition of what she had been saying to herself and the thoughts that held her frozen in failure dawning on her face. Her eyes widened.

"So what is the opposite of a loser—which you are not?" I asked.

"I'm a winner? But I sure don't feel like a winner in my marriage."

I said, "Your marriage doesn't have to be a win/lose situation. It can be a time in your life of great enlightenment. And that's what winners do. In hard times, they look for what they have learned from the experience and use it to grow."

All these moments of self-realization were building Mary Ann's deeper sense of worth, which caused her to continually adjust her Takes.

After we had been working together for a while, Mary Ann said she was ready to face ending her marriage. "I can see how I got myself in this mess. It isn't his fault, and I was doing the best I knew how at the time. But I'm ready to let go."

She developed strategies for how the family would proceed with the business and survive. She let them know how they could support her when she had to tell her husband; she wanted them to be near in case he became angry. Because she did not hate her husband anymore, she did not mind working with him, at least for a while, since she knew he would need assistance with book-keeping and generating new business leads. She could continue to help him until it came time for him to transition from her help to someone else's.

Her family's understanding and acceptance of her decision formed a protective boundary around her. They absorbed her calm, her new plans, and, most of all, her new self-respect. With this prevailing attitude, her husband eventually accepted the way it was going to be.

What was Mary Ann's new TAO?

- Mary Ann's New Take: I have the courage to start our divorce proceedings. I can do this and be considerate in the process.
- Mary Ann's Actions: She found a mediator who helped her and her husband design their agreement. She stayed calm, determined, and cooperative.

- Mary Ann's Outcome: Mary Ann is moving forward with her plans and her life. Everyone around her is cooperating for the good of the family. Mary Ann set the example, and those close to her adopted her attitude.

Mary Ann's story is a compelling example of the power of perception. By addressing your own Take, you can turn a difficult situation into one that will work for you. Study your personal Take—what you repeatedly say to yourself, often unconsciously. Then create a more positive one and *think* it, *say* it, and *write* it down frequently. When you do, your new positive Take will influence your Actions and Outcome, and your challenges will become easier.

When you are living in an authentic, promising Take, your flow will happen without the need to push *or* resist. Whenever you listen to your inner voice and you hear it make a Chicken Little comment like "The sky is falling! The sky is falling!" look for a way to change it into a positive Take. Try saying, "The sky is gorgeous! I'm ready for a great day!"

No one wants to feel like the sky is falling. And no one wants to stay stuck in hopelessness. Your fears, negative thoughts, and judgments may be valid, but they also may be inaccurate or unhelpful. Nudging your Take in a positive direction even a millimeter will change your life. Then you will have control over how you react to your circumstances.

You can start today to look for ways to craft a supportive Take (see the next section for tips). That is the first step along your TAO, and this book is your road map. In the next few chapters, we will look more closely at ways to positively craft your Take. Parts II and III will focus on your Actions and Outcome. In the final section, you will learn how to take what you've learned and move forward, living fully from your TAO. Right now, you may feel that you are going through the fire. But with this book as your guide, you will emerge on the other side stronger, wiser, and more alive than ever.

Suggestions for Crafting a Supportive Take

Listen to your self-talk during the day. What negative opinions about yourself, your former partner, and your breakup do you silently express?

Whatever unkind feedback you are listening to, reframe the thought into something positive. For example, instead of saying, "This is too hard! I can't get through this!" change your thoughts and inner conversations to "I have the strength to face this divorce with dignity and compassion."

Remember a time when someone said something mean-spirited to you about your divorce. How many times have you replayed his or her words in your mind? The danger in focusing on what was said is that each time you remember it, you believe it more. Access your higher self, using whatever method works for you, such as prayer, meditation, or visualization. Then forgive the person. Replace the negative phrase with positive words and thoughts about yourself.

Repeat this phrase three times in a row, at least ten times a day: "I totally love and accept myself. I will be my *best* self throughout this transition." This is especially helpful if you cannot identify your inner negative thoughts. This phrase invalidates the harsh judgments you are unknowingly feeding your spirit.

Part I

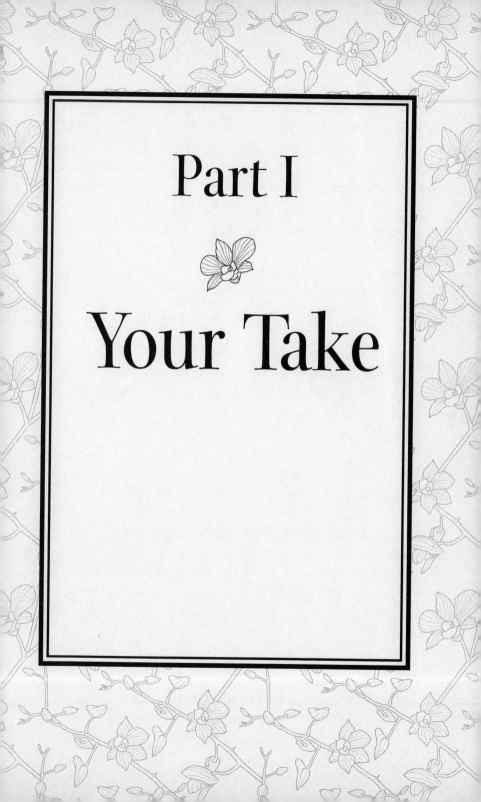

Your Take

2
Laying the Groundwork for Transformation

$\mathcal{A}$ crucial step in formulating your Take is reflecting on what was good from your past with your partner. "Easier said than done," you may be thinking, especially if the pain is still raw. When you are emotionally ready, which may take weeks or months, assessing the positive aspects of your relationship will help you realize the benefits you received from being together. Whatever brought you to a point of leaving each other can be put aside, when appropriate, to allow some appreciation for your joint accomplishments. Pursue this goal in good faith because this is the beginning of your *new* relationship.

When you are fair and kind, your ex will likely reciprocate. You both may be more willing to cooperate in raising children, working together in the family business, or sharing mutual friends. The key to successfully achieving a level of friendship with your partner is to be a role model for how civility can and will be in everyone's best interests. When you do this, you are entering a place of transcendence.

How can you accomplish having a different type of interaction with the person you are breaking up with? What are the skills and processes needed to lay the groundwork for transformation and facilitate a smooth transition into your new life? Here are some suggestions about how to shift your Take and ease into your new relationship with your soon-to-be ex.

Remember that life is often not what it seems or the way you'd thought it would be

When you first met, did your partner seem too good to be true? And then, with the perspective that time and intimacy bring to a relationship, did that perception change? We can make some unbalanced decisions in choosing a mate as a result of our projections and blurred pictures of what we thought we saw. But when we're forced to take another look and realize that things aren't what they had seemed, we may have to make other decisions.

I experienced a small example of this the other day when I was driving in the car with my big dog beside me in the passenger seat. Fresh from the groomer, purple bows in her hair, she was listening while I talked to her. With the sun shining and radio playing, we were enjoying the perfect moment. Then I noticed a cop car following me. Guilt swept over me as I checked my speedometer, but it was only five miles over the limit. *He must be after someone else,* I thought. But sure enough, a few miles down the road, his blue lights went on. I was so in denial that I kept on driving . . . until he turned on his siren. After we had both pulled off to the side, he strode to the car and peered inside while I nervously looked up at him. He staggered back in surprise and said, "Oh . . . that's . . . that's just a *big poodle!*" His face turned crimson red. Embarrassed, he explained that he had thought the "lady" sitting next to me wasn't wearing her seat belt. He closed his ticket book and backed away from the car, telling us to have a nice day. "Raji," I said, turning to my dog, "you almost got me in trouble. We may have to lose the bows."

How often have any of us made this kind of mistake? Based on how someone looks, we jump to conclusions. We project onto them all kinds of attitudes, history, stories, virtues, mystery, and even wrongdoing. But what we perceive is not necessarily reality.

What ideals and delusions did you bring to your partnership? Did you fall for the way your guy looked? Or did she seem to be the nicest person in the world? More importantly, did you think all your loneliness would disappear when you got married? Did you expect to have the perfect home and the ideal family? Did you think you would both feel the same way about each other forever? It's hard to let go of illusions. But being forced to see the way things are instead of the way you wanted them to be is important in forming a clearheaded Take and a big step in growth.

Accept the way things are

The following questions may help you find some clarity around the dissolution of your relationship:

When you met your partner, what beliefs did you have about him or her and the life you wanted?

How did those beliefs turn out? If they were illusions, what made them vanish?

Before you married, were there needs that you were trying to have met? What were they?

Are those needs still there, or did you outgrow them? If you outgrew those needs, did your need for your partner diminish?

What were your values when you met your partner?

Did you have values that your partner lacked and that made it impossible for you to continue the relationship?

After thinking about these questions, are you now ready to face the reality of the way things are never going to be—and accept the way things are?

At the heart of many relationship troubles is the false expectation that one partner has of changing the other. The above questions may assist you in seeing that the desire for the other one to change is often illogical and impossible to achieve, and it lays the foundation for finding "fault." The person you married was probably always just as he is now, but you couldn't see it. Fear, needs, and your "pictures" of the way you thought he was or the way you wanted him to be got in the way.

Expecting a "correct" type of behavior from your partner in the future can block the progress to civility. Couples become stuck in thinking there is a "right way" or a "wrong way" to act in a relationship—and then in a divorce. Without one or both people taking responsibility for a cordial approach to the breakup, battle lines are drawn, sides are taken, and everyone the divorce impacts digs deeper in the trenches. When you accept the reality of your relationship not working and allow both of you to be just the way you are, you have opened up new lines of communication. It might not happen immediately, but when it does, it will be possible to set aside blame.

Be civil at all times

You may have moments—or days—of anger, but whenever you interact with your ex, her family, your joint co-workers, or your mutual friends, try to rise above those feelings of rage and conduct yourself with dignity. Losing your temper in front of others is the way you betray yourself. If you abandon your spiritual self and resort to a childlike state of acting out, you will feel controlled and victimized. When you respond with civility, you are in a state of grace.

Always take the high road. Whenever you are experiencing difficult emotions, make them work for you instead of against you. Use that energy as a positive source to do something that is good for you. Find other ways to release anger or resentment, such as venting to a close friend, participating in sports, working out at the gym, or finding creative outlets like painting, sculpting, dancing, or gardening.

Stay away from unresolved emotional issues

When you talk with your ex, minimize the hard times and hard feelings. Look for conversations that cover common ground. Stay away from discussions that revisit old issues that were never resolved.

If you feel seized with negativity toward him, stop and look at your own life. What are you angry about? Did you want your ex to provide for you better? Did you want him to give you more money, more love, or more time? Did you want a deeper level of understanding? Now ask yourself this: When did you give these to yourself?

Often, the emotions and acts of love that we desperately want from others are those we could be giving ourselves. Do you think you aren't competent enough to be financially successful? Of course you are. Just because you haven't found your niche or your talent doesn't mean it isn't there. It could provide you with financial reward.

Do you want more love? When was the last time you asked your friends to tell you what you mean to them? And if you don't have any friends, perhaps that is your next learning curve—how to make and sustain friendships.

Do you want to be listened to and heard? When was the last time you listened to yourself? Do you give yourself what you need? Your higher self sends you messages when you are longing for comfort or emotional food; listen to your inner wisdom so you can provide some of your own needs.

In all cases of disappointment, discover what you have not done for *you*. Then set goals to achieve what you are missing. You'll find more success by trying to meet your own needs than by dwelling on what was left unfulfilled by your former partner.

Don't ask children or in-laws to take sides

If you are tempted to persuade your children or your ex's family that you are without fault or responsibility for the breakup of your relationship, you're traveling down the wrong road. Relationships are mutual. When you break up, you both had some part in it. But who was right and who was wrong are irrelevant to the future of your new and different relationships with your ex and the extended family.

If you engage in "ex-bashing," you'll regret it. Children especially need a community of people to raise them. It is in your best interest, and theirs, not only to have people love your children but also to introduce them to different situations, experiences, and perspectives. Children also need to know their history from both sides of the family. The familial attention and identity awareness that families bring to children are essential to helping them feel grounded and that they "belong."

If you complain to your in-laws about your ex, they will only withdraw from you. Forget about what should have, could have, and would have been better if only he or she had acted differently.

Strive to allow your extended family to remain friendly with you or on safe ground when you are in their presence. If you don't ask them to take sides, they can remain cooperative.

Keep the focus on healing

You may no longer have romance in your relationship, but you can heal yourself to the point where you can have a friendship. Often, the person who was "left" is the one who has a harder time getting over the breakup. If you are the one who initiated the divorce, give your ex time to gain some perspective. Do not expect too much of the person too soon. Keep a clear boundary so he or she does not confuse your kindness with the potential of reigniting the romance.

If you are the one who was left, do not cling to your partner. Clinging causes more resistance and pushes people away. If he wants to leave, let him go with open arms. What is it you are trying to avoid by hanging on? Whatever it is, be honest with yourself and face it. If he doesn't want to be there, you don't want him to remain. Exercise self-love. Choose to be with only those people who want to be with you.

Stay appropriate in conversations and don't discuss your social life

Even if you and your ex establish a caring friendship, it is best not to share your personal dating details. This isn't an appropriate subject. Should it be brought up for any reason, keep it light and keep it general. If you don't want to spark hurt feelings, if you don't want to bring up any subconscious feelings of jealousy between you, and if you want to support all chances for a cordial relationship, then don't share your dating stories.

Practice forgiveness

Forgiveness is the best thing you can do for yourself, whether you were the one leaving or you were the one left. Start by forgiving yourself for your part in the breakup. Continue the process by asking for forgiveness from your ex and by forgiving your ex. If you don't feel strong enough to do this face-to-face, write a letter. If you feel he or she will not understand what you are saying or may misconstrue your meaning, don't mail it. Instead, pretend the person is in a chair in front of you and read it aloud. List everything you would like to express but are afraid to say in person. When you do this, you will feel an enormous burden lift from your shoulders.

Losing Self-Deception and Gaining Acceptance

It's impossible to transition into a new life when you are fighting the change required. Here's how one of my clients made her shift.

When Gretchen first came to see me, she was thin, drawn, and tense. She revealed that she hadn't been taking care of herself and felt guilty about starting to smoke again. Married for twenty-five years to a guy she'd dated in college, she had a son ready to graduate from high school. After her husband had destroyed their business, she threw him out, filed for divorce, and stayed in bed for a year, crying.

She cried because she did not know how to take care of herself. She cried because she didn't have any friends. And, most of all, she cried because she wanted him to come back and take care of her—in all the ways that he never had.

Gretchen did not know how to make the necessary shift into being a single divorced woman. Essentially, she wanted to stay the same even though she knew she was living a lie. She was caught in a negative circular pattern. Her Take was negative, her Actions were self-destructive, and her Outcome was always more bad news, which reconfirmed her negative thoughts about herself and the world. This is exactly how the TAO of divorce works—in a negative spiral.

Gretchen had started a business when she was young, run it successfully for more than ten years, and then turned it over to her husband. But eight years ago, her husband began to incur financial losses—a fact he did not share with her. Instead, he tried to cover it up by charging them to their credit cards. Only when he had maxed out the cards and borrowed all he could from the bank did he tell her.

Gretchen was ashamed to tell her family, but in the end, her older sister came to their financial rescue, paying off all the loans and cards. Gretchen's husband swore he'd never be that irresponsible again.

Wanting to believe she could trust him, Gretchen went on sticking her head in the sand. She isolated herself socially and spent the next seven years cooking, gardening, painting, and decorating—and staying out of their finances. She was completely devastated, of course, when the bank called her and asked for a mortgage payment. They told her it hadn't been paid in three months.

Gretchen felt lonely and abandoned. She also felt betrayed by her husband's lying, secrecy, and cheating. She felt that her son took his father's side whenever she talked about him, and that her son didn't understand how much she had been hurt. What Gretchen couldn't yet see, until she grew stronger, was that she had abandoned herself long ago in the marriage.

"I must have been so totally stupid not to have paid attention to what was going on," Gretchen told me. "Now I'm in this place where I haven't worked in years. I don't know what to do, where to go, or how to support myself. I feel completely worthless." She was hostage to her negative Take.

I told her, "Instead of focusing on what you think is wrong with you, let's look at what is *right* with you. From everything you've told me about your life, it sounds like you are an artistic person. That strength can work for you or against you.

"You used your talents to distract yourself from seeing the red flags in your relationship. No one runs a business into debt without warning signs popping up. You must have kept yourself very busy to have not seen the flags. Your art projects provided an excuse to be preoccupied so you wouldn't notice."

"But why didn't he tell me the truth?" she cried.

I responded with a question. "What was the truth about your marriage that you didn't want to face?"

"That I was disappointed in my husband and so was my family. So I just stayed busy and tried not to think about it."

"Everyone has the capacity to get off track in their lives," I said. "This is especially true when you don't want to see something."

"I don't know what to do now. I'm not sure I have any strengths," Gretchen said.

I told her, "Of course you do! You're going to call upon your creative spirit, your good intentions to always do the best that you can, and the financial and marketing savvy you had when you ran your business. You can also take your nurturing qualities and turn them toward you. Give yourself what you want, instead of looking to a relationship to deliver it."

Gretchen's transformation required that she stay focused on the strengths that would help her take care of herself. She made a list of her skills, talents, and experience. This helped her see that when she said, "I don't know how to do anything," she was actually telling herself a lie—and that lie kept her stuck. She started taking some action steps that would put her life in motion.

Next, we identified her negative Take and rewrote it. She stopped repeating and reaffirming, "I'm so dumb! I don't know *what* I'm going to do." She changed it to "I'm smart and competent. I'll find what I love to do and take care of myself." The truth and hope in that statement energized her and redirected her thoughts and beliefs.

It didn't take Gretchen long to determine that she wanted to be a decorator. While she began to set up her business, she took a part-time job at an art gallery. Now she had some money coming in and a budding career she was excited about.

How did she do it? Gretchen found ten other decorators on the internet who had similar tastes to hers. She asked them how they got started, what they charged, and how long it took to have a full-time business. She discovered the pitfalls, the ways to success, and how to manage her client base. Networking with people in her community, she let them know what she was doing. She gave presentations at women's groups, visited shops and left her business card, and talked to real estate agents for referrals. She found and implemented new marketing ideas each week. Staying in bed all day crying was no longer an option.

Gretchen's business started to grow. She quit smoking, started riding her bike, and reconnected with old friends as she began to make new ones.

When Gretchen stopped blaming her husband for her unhappiness, she saw a different relationship with him emerging. She said she would never be good friends with him, but she could be civil. Finally, she was able to sign the divorce papers.

When it was time to send her son off to college, she was actually able to sit down with her ex and talk about what they needed to do to get him ready. She found that they could have friendly conversations about their son's future. Thankfully, she no longer wanted or needed her son to take sides.

She said, "My husband and I both agreed that we are proud of our son. He was the best gift from our marriage. We are very supportive of each other when we talk about him."

Gretchen found it easier than she had thought it would be to attend her son's graduation, hug her former in-laws, go to dinner with the extended family, and drive her son to college with her ex. She said the entire experience was calm. Neither of them felt any compulsion to talk about the past or bring up the issues that always gave them problems.

Shortly after she signed the papers for the divorce, one of her friends told her that she had seen Gretchen's ex out on a date. But Gretchen didn't feel compelled to ask him about it. She had let go.

Gretchen successfully laid a foundation for transformation, beginning by seeing the reality of her situation and no longer deceiving herself. With eyes wide open, she formed a constructive Take. From there, her positive Actions moved her toward an Outcome that benefitted herself, her son, her former husband, and their extended family. Her TAO brought her to a new way of being— one that honored the past but stayed firmly focused on the future.

Each relationship has its own life span. In yours, you came together to learn from each other. Your partner represents some aspect of yourself that you longed to heal, understand, or affirm. Sometimes you are together long enough to enjoy one another and learn before you move into another part of your life. Some relationships are meant to last forever and some are not.

Relationships change, and it is important to recognize that in the case of breaking up, change is not rejection. Change is a natural flow—the TAO of divorce. That is why you can't hang on when someone wants to go and why you cannot let yourself be made to feel guilty if you don't want to stay any longer.

Thank your ex-partner for what you've learned—and say good-bye to the way it used to be.

Suggestions for Transitioning to a New Relationship with Your Ex

When it is clear that the romance is over but you still want or need to have a relationship, make a list of the good that came from your partnership. What are you grateful for? Stay focused on the positive, resisting the temptation to rehash the bad. You can do this alone, or together when the time is right. You can also suggest that both of you make lists and email them to each other.

When you feel the situation is appropriate, share the vision you have for your new relationship. Rescript how, where, and when you will interact. What must be different in your behavior toward each other for you both to remain friendly? Talk about how to respect each other's privacy, limitations, and expectations.

Write notes to mutual friends and former in-laws you care about and build a new bridge to them from your emerging independent self. Tell them what you appreciated about them in the past and that you look forward to continuing a friendship with them in the future.

Make a list of what you want to change in yourself when relating to your ex. Gather some close friends and ask them for feedback about your behavior. How do you react and interact with her that is not in your best interests? What behaviors have become habits that you have the power to change? What emotional safety zones, mental pictures, or states of mind do you need when you see him? Make a list of what you think might work and try some of them.

Visualize the friendship you would like to have with your ex. Knowing your partner's characteristics, keep it realistic as well as positive. Every morning when you wake up and every night before you fall asleep, visit that image. See it, feel it, and hold that vision until it is a reality.

3
Taking Stock

*N*ow that you have laid the groundwork for transformation, it's time for the next step along your TAO. Before you re-enter the world in your new role of being single, you must set aside a resting point and take stock.

Why is quiet, reflective time so important now? Because only through an honest assessment of what you take from the past, where you are now, and where you are headed can you develop the Take that leads to the Actions and Outcome you desire. Now, while the end of the relationship is still fresh, you can shape the path of your future and bring it about with fewer bumps along the way.

The challenge is that being still at this stage may feel counter-intuitive. When you are coming out of a relationship, you may unconsciously be looking for rescue. You may be tempted to throw yourself into a new relationship, stay in bed and hide under the covers, or fill your days and nights with too much to do, staying frantically busy. Any of these pursuits will send you off course and hinder your transformation.

In order to take care of yourself, whether managing what you have or what you've got to go and get, sooner or later you have to be still and look inward. You have to ask yourself, What is it I really, really, *really* want ... and what do I have to do to get it? Until you have faced this truth, distractions will invade your life and you will be vulnerable to false comfort.

This is the perfect moment to assess your skills and strengths and look at how you might use some of them in your future. Start by affirming what you know. It's time to assess where you are. When you married, you probably had some strengths and talents you may have forgotten during the course of your relationship. And even though some of them may have been set aside during that time, others may have grown stronger.

One thing is certain: you are not the same person now that you were when you met your ex. You are wiser, you have grown, and you know things you didn't know then. You have arrived at this juncture with additional skills and the opportunity to activate any talents you have not been using in order to create the life you want.

In this chapter, I'll guide you in identifying whatever you have felt was missing from your life that you now want to develop and experience. Whether it is the ability to be financially independent, create your own home, find a new career, make new friends, or start tap-dancing lessons, it's time to take stock of your needs.

Regaining Financial Freedom

For me, my most pressing need on the heels of my divorce was financial. This stage of my "growth by divorce" was the worst time—and the best worst time—of my life. I awoke one morning to the reality of my situation. I was alone, child support was non-existent, I had no job, money, or family near, and I had cosigned loans and credit cards that had to be paid. Frozen in fear, I wondered how I would take care of my children and keep a roof over our heads.

The children were constantly asking for things, and I was constantly replying, "We can't buy that. I don't have the money."

My four-year-old had the perfect solution: "Go to the bank, Mommy. They have lots of money. They'll give you some."

The debt was mounting, and I knew I had to do something. It was time to take stock. I needed a job—fast! I had once been a teacher in another state, but I wasn't certified in the state where I lived. Further, a teaching job wouldn't pay enough to live on *and* pay off all the debts. Educational consulting was too sporadic and involved travel. I looked into sales, but there was not enough base pay in the positions offered. I searched job listings, went to dozens of interviews, and finally thought I had landed a job as a director of a federally funded educational program. Out of more than five hundred people who had applied, I made the cut to the top three. Using all my intention and visualization, I just knew I'd get the job. Finally, they called—and I didn't get it.

Wild with worry, I did another checklist of my skills. It seemed like a weird idea, but I remembered that when I was a consultant, I had taught a workshop the teachers loved. It was in creative dance, music, and movement—something I had developed from my imagination and from working with kids. Maybe I could start my own business in an after-school program for children.

I hustled. Time was running out. My children and I made posters advertising the classes. We hung them on the walls in shopping centers and grocery stores. We handed out flyers after church, and I took advantage of free advertising in neighborhood papers and community bulletin boards. I went to different churches around town and asked to rent their halls. Many of the pastors, once they saw my classes, said I didn't need to pay rent because I was "doing God's work." Who knew?

Stranger yet, my phone started to ring. I filled four afternoon schools in four different parts of town in less than a month. Monday through Thursday, I was teaching forty-five kids a day.

The director of a school for emotionally challenged children saw one of my posters and asked to hire me for two days a week to do my dance program for them. They gave me a salary *and* health insurance.

After a year, I applied for and received a grant to do my program with physically handicapped children one day a week, and I got funded for four years. Emotionally and physically challenged children often can't take regular dance classes, but they could thrive in the specially designed classes I was offering, which incorporated movement, expression, music, singing, stories, and costumes.

Newspapers did profiles on my inventive schools, I became a regular on a noon TV talk show, and I was asked to perform at festivals. Women's groups, therapists, school systems, parents, and others wanted classes, concerts, or workshops. It's hard to believe it as I look back, but I had reinvented myself as a "singer and musician," which was a stretch for me. Soon I was making recordings for children and writing books to go with them.

It took four years to pay off the debt I had been left with. I bartered, giving dance classes to some children in exchange for their parents' services: accounting, home repair, car services, Spanish and art lessons for my kids, and a truckload of flowers and plants each year from a nursery owner.

Neighbors and friends could see my struggle and offered help and support along the way. I was ashamed of my predicament, but my growing success lifted some of that burden. Years after I crawled out of the hole I was in, people would tell me what an inspiration I had been to them during their times of pain or disintegrating marriages. I had had no idea!

This immense challenge gave me something no job ever has. I learned that if the whole world around me fell apart, I could still figure out how to survive. That confidence is still with me.

My Take from that experience was that I always have choices, but being a victim is not one of them.

I also learned that I could get myself in an emotional and financial mess in the blink of an eye. But when I created a life I was proud of, one that became precious to me, I wasn't so likely to slip into a bad relationship and toss it all away. I realized that whatever I had been trying to hide from by getting married was not as scary as what I had just gone through. Ultimately, I had learned to rescue myself.

When a breakup requires a change in how you make a living, it's time to take stock of your talents. You may be looking for a new direction for the rest of your life. Or, like me, you may simply be looking for a way to survive. Taking stock requires you to recognize everything you know how to do, even if some things seem insignificant. As my experience shows, with enough imagination you can turn any talent into an income stream.

Finding a New Direction

Sometimes it's the skills you take for granted that are exactly what others need in their lives. This was the case with my client Angie, who needed to find a new direction in her life after her divorce left her with little self-confidence and self-respect.

Angie was a stunning young woman with no children. She had always assumed that a man would take care of her, since she had no trouble attracting anyone she wanted. But when her husband left her for a model, her world crashed. "I hate my ex for leaving me for someone younger and prettier," she said.

She lamented that she had never been trained for any kind of work and had no skills. She wanted to get married again, and I asked her what she wanted her life to look like if she didn't find anyone to marry.

"Well, I could never work in an office. I don't know how to use a computer, and I would hate sitting still and going to the same place every day. I think that a boring job where you are not important is the thing I would hate the most. I didn't go to college, and it's hard for me to think of what I could possibly do. I like helping people, but I don't know in what capacity I would do that."

She continued, "I need someone to take care of me. I'm lonely and I'm anxious to meet a new guy."

I asked her, "Who is this person who is waiting to be taken care of? Who would you like to be?"

"I think I'd like to be Oprah."

"What is it about Oprah that you admire?" I asked.

"She has the perfect life because she gets to do whatever she wants to do."

"What keeps you from doing whatever you'd like to do?"

She thought for a minute and then said, "I don't really know how to take care of myself, and it's too late to get started in learning how to do it."

"And that's why you think you need to marry someone? Because you believe you can't ever excel at anything and it's impossible to learn new skills? Do you understand how that perception is tying you down to hopelessness and keeping you from discovering your own wonderful self . . . not to mention your perfect life?"

She nodded. "I guess I didn't think there was anything about me that was worth discovering."

I said, "When you don't honor yourself and work to become who you want to be, that reluctant behavior also keeps you 'safe.' You don't have to try, perhaps fail sometimes the way most of us do, and try again."

She looked surprised. "When I think about being able to take care of myself, I start to feel excited."

"Tell me something you really love to do," I said. "What did you do as a child that held your attention so deeply that you never wanted to stop doing it?"

She hesitated, seeming embarrassed. "I guess what I liked more than anything was to go over to my friends' houses, go in their rooms, close the door . . . and straighten their closets."

Angie liked organizing drawers, closets, desks, cabinets, and spaces of all kinds. But not until she took stock of her talents did she see that what she kept hidden as her "weird habit" could be a profession. She created a career as a professional organizer, which motivated her to take some computer and accounting classes. No longer a "kept" woman, Angie was moving on. She didn't view herself in the same way she used to and didn't need her looks as her bargaining capital anymore.

After Angie found her self-respect, the day arrived when she couldn't remember that she used to hate her husband. She said they weren't exactly friends, since he had remarried, but they certainly weren't enemies anymore.

What was Angie's new Take? Self-respect is something you earn— by doing a good job, trying hard, facing your fears, and taking care of yourself. No one gives it to you; it's something you give yourself.

After you determine what you want to do, tell everyone about it. They might not know they need it until they hear of it.

Creating a Social Network

Everyone has different issues to adjust to when their partnership dissolves. Mine happened to be financial as well as emotional,

but you may have different ones, as was the case with my client
Thomas.

Entering social activities after a divorce or breakup can be
stressful and even scary. This is how Thomas took stock of his
social life and turned it around.

Thomas was devastated when his wife left him for his friend,
who was also his investment broker. He felt especially lost and
isolated since his wife had been the social hub of their life. She
had organized their parties, had people over for dinner, planned
their trips with their children and friends, kept in touch with
family members, volunteered for charitable organizations, and
seemed to have her finger on the pulse of the community.

When she left, Thomas said, he was completely alone. Most
of their mutual friends gravitated to her and her new life. Even
their children spent most of their time with their mother.
Thomas had his career and money handled (although he did get a
new investment advisor), but he had zero connections to other
people and didn't know where to begin.

Thomas needed to take stock, since he had deferred to his wife
when it came to their social calendar. He had allowed her to be in
charge of whom they saw and whom they didn't see. This is a
problem when you delegate someone to be your recreation director. He had lost touch with old friends, had not paid attention to
who was emotionally available to him in his past and present, and
was clueless as to who was out there for him. Slowly, we began to
uncover people he hadn't thought about in a long time.

He began to list people he wanted to see. His office manager,
a kind, older woman who had worked with him for years, came to
mind. He said that his partner in his firm and his partner's wife, a
couple of professors he had known in college, his mother and brothers, some grad school roommates, and his doctor were all important
to him, even though he had never expressed that to them.

Thomas made a plan to go to dinner with, visit, call, or write to all of them, depending on where they were. He began to make regularly scheduled visits to see his mother and brothers, who lived several thousand miles away. The visits restored him. Later, when he was comfortable with the idea, he let his office manager help him plan a party he hosted at his home. He also began to have lunch once a week with his partner and play tennis on the weekend with his doctor. Thomas started to feel connected.

Then we looked at interests he had not acted upon. At first resistant to the idea, he finally began to talk about taking cooking classes, sailing lessons, and a college course in history. As soon as he did this, Thomas began to exude more energy for his life. He met even more friends in his classes.

Six months later, Thomas's friends were fixing him up with dates. He soon had his own world of people and activities. When he learned to make friends on his own, it was easier to be around his ex and the friends they once had in common. In fact, Thomas is amazed at how calm he is around his ex and her husband. They are all on friendly terms.

What's Thomas's new Take? I never have to be alone unless I choose to be. When I take the necessary steps to reach out to others, I have friends.

Time to Take Stock

As the previous examples show, breaking up requires change. Even if your career, hobbies, and friends remain unchanged, certain aspects of your life may require major adjustments. Your standard of living may need to change; your identity may need reexamining; your dreams for the future may have to be totally rewritten. Change becomes easier when you look at your past, present, and future from a different perspective. Here are some guidelines for doing just that:

Focus on what you carry with you from your past relationship

What was the good that came out of your relationship? Think about the person you were before your relationship began. You were no doubt a very different person from who you are today. In what ways have you improved in terms of your personality, knowledge, wisdom, skills, and talents? What do you know today that you didn't know before? How can you use this new knowledge?

Almost all my clients, men and women, had been married to someone who had brought them new information, ideas, and experiences.

One woman had been married to a doctor who needed help sorting out the insurance forms for his patients. Working alongside his staff, she had learned how to navigate the insurance companies' claims filing system. When they divorced, she found it possible to get a job in this area.

One man learned about photography from his ex. He now has a hobby he is crazy about. He told me that when they first got divorced, it was the one thing that gave him solace.

Another man had helped his wife set up her catering business, learning about the necessary equipment, tax forms, certifications, and health codes. When their relationship ended, helping others set up this kind of work became his new hobby and contribution.

Many of my male clients said that they learned to cook from their ex. They said they eat healthier meals now than they had before the relationship.

Other clients learned new skills in accounting, computer technology, sales, publishing, and advertising media that they would never have been exposed to if they had not been with the person they had married. Almost all their acquired knowledge that came from their past relationships became useful in their new lives. Whatever you learned in your partnership, it can be redirected to a new use, an exciting hobby, a different career, or a new life's purpose.

Eliminate negative thoughts you have about yourself as you start to create your new life

Many of my clients have said they have some of the following thoughts:

I don't have the right skills. You probably have many talents you aren't even aware of. Do you garden, decorate, bake, or do carpentry? If there are skills you need to start a new business, you can always take classes to learn them. If you don't have all the abilities you want, you can learn some new ones.

I'm too old to start over. Never buy into this one. For many people, this excuse has little to do with age and is more an expression of regret over wasted time. Age or a feeling of lost time shouldn't stand between you and the life you want. My mother started riding and competing in the rodeo when she was fifty . . . and she was terrified of horses. It's never too late to meet new people, relocate across the country, or get involved in an activity you enjoy!

I'm no longer attractive/I can't compete. If you are judging yourself from the outside, it may be true that your body and face have changed. That's a reality. What you are forgetting, however, is to acknowledge the wisdom you've gained, the humanity you've developed, and the lessons you've learned. The more you allow that experience to surface, the more attractive you become.

I don't have a college degree. Many people who are extremely successful did not go to college. They learned how to do what they do "on the job" or from a mentor. And if you want to go to college, you can start at any time. There are many ways to get an education or finish what you may have already started. Consider taking classes at your community college, taking courses online, or getting a tutor. You have at your disposal many sources and people who would love to help you.

I don't have a purpose. We all have to start somewhere. Think about your interests and an organization that represents them; then get your foot in the door, starting as a volunteer. This will be a good place to find meaningful work and meet people who share your interests.

No one will hire me because I don't have the right experience. You are probably discounting the experience you do have, even if you weren't paid for it. If you totaled up all your hours of work unrelated to a formal job, it would amount to a lot. Find ways to reframe it in conversations and in a résumé to reflect what you know. Many people leave one profession and enter another that is completely unrelated, yet they list the skills they've acquired in a way that will apply to the new job.

I don't know anyone in this area. Ask yourself what you can do to get out into the community and introduce yourself to people. Many organizations would welcome your presence—

all you have to do is seek them out. Find one that is dedicated to one of your interests, such as animal shelters, groups
that feed the homeless, hospital volunteers, parents without
partners, the chamber of commerce, or environmental
organizations.

Look for the lie in your belief that says you can "never" do anything. It is that lie that keeps you from achieving your goal. Pay
attention to what you are telling yourself and others. All the above
are simply convoluted reasons you give yourself to not try.

How do you find the lie? By asking yourself, "Where is the evidence to support this statement? Where is the proof that shows I
can't make my life better?" Ask yourself these questions and you'll
see there is nothing to support your self-limiting beliefs.

Design your days to be successful

Imagine your perfect day. Write it all down. Capture how it smells,
feels, tastes, sounds, and looks. What would you be doing if you
had your choice?

Make a list of what you can take from your perfect-day essay
and put it into your current life. Make another list of the steps to
take to create some of the other qualities. At the end of each day,
remember what you did right, what you did well, what you
accomplished, and what you can look forward to doing tomorrow.

Move from complaints to solutions

It is easy to fall into a negative pit and obsess about everything
that went "wrong." If you have a tendency to think in that vein,
use those thoughts to help you make a list of everything you do
not want to do. This list will move you to what you *do* want.

What has kept you from realizing your own criteria for success and identifying what you want?

If you want something but you do not take action and work hard for it, you may be experiencing ambivalence. You may not be able to move one way or the other. What are the payoffs from that behavior? Does being helpless get you sympathy, love, or attention?

What other factors might be holding you back from your dreams? Are you rebelling, stubborn, or feeling guilty? Are you up against cultural assumptions or conflicting desires? Take an inventory of the inner voices and attitudes that are holding you hostage and then rephrase them.

Taking Stock Assessment

This exercise can help you get a clear picture of where you are. Take out a notebook or journal to write freely about the thoughts that the following questions raise. Add other questions that apply to your life.

1. What did your partner provide you with that you think you cannot achieve on your own? Money? Family? Friends? Home? Career? Status? Social Skills? Something else?

   What steps can you take to give yourself what you need or want? What can you do to shift self-defeating attitudes about the above areas?

2. What "*shoulds*" can you let go of (as in "I should do ...," "I should be ...," "I should have ...")?

3. What are your talents? List all you can think of.

4. What classes, lessons, mentoring, or experiences have you had that bring you a unique perspective?

5. What do you dislike doing?

6. What do you love to do?

7. Whom would you most like to be? Why?

8. What qualities does that person you admire have?

9. What characteristics and strengths of this person can you start to show more of in your life now?

10. What do your friends and family come to you for? What do you do that they value?

11. What were you doing when you were most proud of yourself?

12. What do other people admire about you or compliment you on?

13. What do you do well that you think is so simple that anyone could do it?

Reflect on these questions, and soon a river of ideas will start flowing. You will shift from a self-limiting Take to one that acknowledges all your abilities and possibilities. See this moment as an opportunity—and act on it.

The dissolution of your relationship is your big motivator to stop and take stock. Reinventing yourself is not only possible; it's an ongoing, healthy process. Whatever you have been putting off or avoiding or not wanting to think about in terms of your present and future, now is the time to assess what you can do. Put all your skills, strengths, experience, training, and ideas for making your life better down on paper and out in front of you. It is then that you can see what you have going for you and what more you need.

The entire process of taking stock may seem insignificant, tedious, or boring, but it's actually a great opportunity. After all, when's the last time you did a survey of everything you know? And what have you thought about doing for yourself in the past that would require you to take some new action that could change your life? These are the measures that move you to where you want to be.

Suggestions for Taking Stock

Find a quiet place and time to close your eyes and picture where you would like to be and what you would like to be doing. Repeat this process several times a day.

Call five people who know you well and ask them:

- When do they remember you being happiest in your life?
- What did they always see you doing?
- What goals do they remember you expressing?
- What makes you important to them?

Write down their answers and the insight this exercise gave you.

Go back and take another look at the "Taking Stock Assessment" section on pages 42–44.

- What did you learn that surprised you?
- What did you remember that you could do, that you had forgotten about?
- What were you glad to be reminded of?
- What do you want to do more of?
- What new skills are you ready for?

Now that you've taken stock, what is your new Take on the life you want to create?

4
Strengthening Your Boundaries

You may not believe it, especially if you have gone through a bitter and difficult breakup, but there are hidden treasures under the fragments of your divorce. As I mentioned in the introduction, the TAO, or the way, of divorce is a process that works through you. At this stage of your development, the unresolved challenges between you and your former partner may look like the rocky sediment at the end of a receding glacier. But in fact, when you put light on what seemed like debris, you'll be able to see the glimmer of insight.

The blessings and revelations from your former relationship are immeasurably valuable in forming your Take. When you observe your past through a different lens, you will be able to see how you want to structure your future. What could be more important than that?

So how *do* you create a divorce that's peaceful when there is so much potential for disharmony? What can you do to find a new way to look at the issues you have struggled with in your relationship, to get the wisdom that can be found there?

The most important resource you need is *boundaries*.

When you grasp the power of boundaries and develop the mastery to use them effectively, nothing will ever look the same again. You need boundaries now, when you are stretching to find the best way to relate to your ex, your former in-laws, your co-joined business colleagues, and your mutual friends.

Boundaries are actually not foreign to us. We learn about them throughout our lives. We're just not always aware of how to use them to take care of ourselves. When we start to understand them, we remember many situations where a boundary set needed parameters in place.

One autumn, I went home for Thanksgiving. Nearing our house, I could smell the familiar scent of my father's stockyard mingling with the crisp November air. I stepped into the house and was greeted with the familiar aromas from my mother's kitchen, which I inhaled deeply to savor. My sister and mother were putting the finishing touches on dinner, and my eyes feasted on the traditional holiday fare: candied yams, mashed potatoes, hot rolls, dressing, cranberry sauce, and . . . what was that? Was that stringy, grizzled, buzzard-like carcass lying on the platter supposed to be a turkey?

I knew better than to say anything to my mother, so I took my sister aside and asked, "What's the matter with the turkey?"

She confided, "Remember that old rooster that fell off someone's truck a long time ago? It'd been out in the driveway walking around with the dogs for five or six years. Mother decided to save some money this year. She cooked it."

Now that made perfect sense. Mother had lived through the Oklahoma dust bowl Depression-era years, and she had some strange frugal ways. We all sat down to dinner, none of us saying anything when she put the bird on the table. But when my father's eyes finally rested on it, he looked horrified and confused at the same time. He looked at the bird; he looked at my mother; he looked back at the bird. Finally, he said, "Alma? Did this turkey have a disease?"

She politely said, "No," but there was a look in her eyes that also said, "End of discussion." Which it was, because we were too busy chewing . . . and chewing.

What I know now that I didn't understand then is that not only did my mother have her own eccentric ways of saving money, but she also had a strong set of boundaries around her values. There were some lines you just didn't cross, and we all knew not to cross that one.

What does this mean for you when you are going through a divorce? You need to know how to draw those specific, important lines with others. You draw that line with your words, your gestures, and your attitude that says, "Don't cross!"

Without boundaries, you will keep creating the same level of response from people, which shows up in their demands, expectations, or attitudes toward you. This is especially true in a close relationship with a partner. When you are going through a breakup, boundaries will be your best protection from increased hurt or misunderstandings.

Types of Boundaries

What are those lines and what do they look like? There are four types of boundaries—*interior, exterior, proactive,* and *reactive*—that will take care of you forever. In this chapter we'll look at each one in depth, as well as how to get them to work for you.

Interior Boundaries

Interior boundaries are the inner messages given to you by your body, mind, and spirit. They are there to inform you when you are falling out of balance and need to take better care of yourself. The key is to be able to *recognize* the message, which can take the form of physical symptoms, negative thoughts, and uneasy feelings—all signs that you are out of balance.

How do you get out of balance? If you are going through a divorce, getting out of balance is easy. During this time, you can become more vulnerable to your own negative thoughts, as well as suggestions or pressures from others. Responsibilities, demands, and requests can crowd you. Clients come to me saying that they feel overwhelmed and their lives are spinning out of control. They cannot find the time to enjoy some quiet moments of reflection.

You need times of rest and silence to build your strength. Being out of balance with your inner self does not contribute to a clear head, positive energy, or the ability to make good decisions. What are some examples of how this imbalance might get started?

Did your soon-to-be-ex-mother-in-law call and ask you to run some errands for her when you were so tired that you just wanted to go home from work and crawl into bed?

Did your sister ask you to watch her kids for a week?

Has your boss been asking you to work overtime every night, without any compensation?

Did your soon-to-be-ex say you weren't being kind enough to his family?

Did your neighbor call and ask you to divulge all the details of why your relationship was ending?

The easiest way you can get caught up in depleting your energy and falling out of balance is by trying to please everyone and giving them what they want—at your expense.

You may find it hard to say no to some people. However, your expectations of yourself, when you have set the bar too high, can create more stress than is healthy. Trying to meet unreasonable goals, please too many people, and go through a divorce at the same time can leave you feeling like you want to run away.

Answer these questions:

Are you desperate to get a grip on your life?

Does your heart have limits as to how much judgment, scrutiny, or disappointment you can take from those around you?

Are you out of touch with what will feed you because you have been so focused on everyone else's problems?

What can you do, while going through the breakup process, to take better care of yourself?

The answer to all the above is to *listen for your inner voice*. It will tell you when you need to rest, eat, exercise, work, take some time alone, or be with supportive people. This voice will also warn you when your life is in charge of you rather than the other way around. When you don't listen to this knowing voice, you have crossed a boundary within.

How do you recognize the inner voice? It takes practice—especially when you have been tuned in to the demands of others. It's also hard to hear your quiet voice trying to guide you when it is competing with the thunder of your fear. Fear of being alone, not finding a job that pays you enough to live, or being unable to handle life all by yourself can sound like a drumroll growing louder each day.

You can learn to turn up your inner volume, however, once you understand what you are missing and how necessary it is that you *listen*.

Not understanding interior boundaries gave Sally a lot of problems. She came to see me after she was separated from her husband.

When Sally still lived with her husband, she was a pharmaceutical sales rep, traveling a lot and always feeling pressure to make her quotas. Sally spent day and night planning her schedule, making calls, seeing clients, reading about her products, and pushing herself to higher and higher goals. In addition to working to meet her own personal standards, Sally's boss, in-laws, mother, and husband always wanted more and more of her and she would try to deliver.

Physical signs of stress began to appear. Sally would clench her jaw when she slept and experienced chronic headaches as a result. She also lived with tense muscles in her arms, legs, and neck, and would walk around with a knot in her stomach. Sally started to feel like a stretched rubber band, ready to snap.

Sally didn't know how to slow down or get out of the fast lane. She would have coffee for breakfast, dash from one meeting to the next living on doughnuts, and stay up late at least three nights a week having dinner with clients. Sometimes she didn't get to bed until two or three in the morning.

Sally never had time for a conversation with her husband during the week, and if they did manage to fit one in, it often became a fight. He would complain that Sally never did anything for him, that she didn't know how to have fun, and that she made him her last priority. They were always yelling, which made Sally more exhausted.

Sally also was trying to earn enough for them to live on as well as pay off both their student loans. Her husband never seemed to understand that. Sally didn't know where he thought they got the money to survive if she didn't work as hard as she did, since he had a nine-to-five job that didn't pay much.

Sally led this life for three years until one day—completely exhausted—she just couldn't move. After resting for a week and still not feeling any better, Sally went to the doctor. It was mononucleosis. It took her months to get well, and while she was recuperating, her husband left her.

Sally desperately needed to learn about all levels of boundaries—particularly interior boundaries—so that she could take better care of herself. Sally told me, "I never paid attention to what was right or healthy for me, in my work or my marriage. I tried to please everyone, wore myself out, and, in the end, wound up pleasing no one. When my ex left, I was extremely bitter.

"Now I can see that my ex did take advantage of me, but it is also true that I let it happen. I had no boundary in place, so he expected and wanted too much, I expected too much of me, and I let everyone else do the same."

Once Sally felt healthy, strong, and emotionally comfortable with her boundaries, she met her ex at a coffee shop one day to discuss important divorce matters.

She told me, "I needed to talk with him without being sabotaged by the resentment and hurt I used to have. I think a lot of my anger was that he was never going to be as responsible as I wanted him to be. I realize now that we would never be happy together and that we had both married the wrong person."

Sally asked her ex for his forgiveness for not understanding what was happening and for all the times she had screamed at him. To her surprise, he was kind. He apologized too.

Sally's new Take: I will take loving care of my body, emotions, and life because when I don't, no one is served.

This is how the inner messages such as those Sally finally learned to pay attention to will announce themselves:

Cotton balls. The first time a message of warning or knowing is delivered to you, it is as gentle as a cotton ball falling on your head. You may notice it, but unless you are aware of its significance, you don't pay any attention to it. Your wise inner voice is trying to tell you to get some rest, but you may ignore it, press on, and keep working. *Sally never even noticed it.*

Tennis balls. The next time your inner voice tries to get your attention, it has more urgency. It might feel like a tennis ball landing on your head, saying, "Get some rest! You are tired!" However, you might not listen because you don't regard your own opinion, you don't trust your voice, or you put others' needs above yours. Even though you are quite tired and you don't feel too well, you also don't heed the warning. *Metaphorically speaking, Sally rubbed her head, took some aspirin, and kept on going.*

Cannonballs. The next time your inner voice tries to get you to take a protective action, the message may be delivered by a cannonball. It takes the form of a more serious event, accident, or illness. This time, you are forced to rest, and perhaps you will finally examine your behavior because the message has brought your life to a halt. *Sally didn't get the full message of what she was doing to herself when she got mono. It was when her husband left her that she decided to look for the changes she could bring to her life.* Can you think of consequences you suffered in the past when you didn't listen to yourself? If so, you have the advantage of being able to alter your future with your ex, your extended family, and yourself. Life is a lot easier when you notice that the cotton balls falling on your head are trying to tell you something.

Exterior Boundaries

Exterior boundaries are the invisible lines you draw between yourself and others, indicating what is okay with you and what is not. You learn to let people know when to *not* cross a sacred line. (This is the line my mother used when she cooked the rooster.)

Enforce your boundaries. If you are a "pleaser," you will let people cross the line of what is appropriate. Learning to say no is the key to avoiding this. Having boundaries and exercising them in a polite but firm way engenders respect from people. Boundaries are essential for *all* your relationships. Even your best friend is capable of unconsciously taking advantage of you. Without your protective lines, you are capable of ruining all potentially good relationships. But boundaries are especially significant when you are negotiating a new relationship with your ex—and, ultimately, yourself.

If you let your ex cross your exterior boundary, you will feel out of sorts with yourself or mad at him or her, or you'll remember the incident or conversation with a sense of embarrassment. Afterward, you will replay what happened over and over in your mind, accompanied by uneasy feelings.

Once you notice those feelings and physical signs, you can prepare yourself for the next time. You can indicate that your ex has trespassed by giving him a certain look, a frown, a word, or a short sentence like "I don't want to talk about it now," or "Can we schedule a more appropriate time and place to discuss this?"

Here's a simple example: You are having a hair-challenged day. If you see your ex and he says, "Your hair looks terrible," you are ready. You put a boundary in place by saying something like "I know it has had better days, but let's not go there." Your tone of voice and the look on your face indicate that you are not going to explain anything.

You don't have to be rude or angry. If you get defensive, apologetic, or explanatory, you have let him cross your boundary, and you have *allowed* him to make you feel bad.

Central to the concept of boundaries is to not let other people have power over you—power to make you feel uncomfortable; power to make you feel like you owe them an explanation; power to insist that you defend your choices or your decisions. Just say, "I don't want to discuss it." You can be friendly; you can be smiling; but you must say it like you mean it.

Respect others' boundaries. Just as you don't want to let your ex trespass over your limits, it's also important to recognize when you might be violating your ex's lines. Without understanding boundaries, it is easy to swing too far in one direction or the other. Stepping back to see what you are allowing or doing will give you the perspective needed to change your behavior, as in the case of my client Christy.

Christy continually had her feelings hurt. She couldn't understand why her husband didn't treat her the way she treated him. Even though they no longer lived together and were getting a divorce, she baked bread for him, walked his dog, shopped for his groceries, did his laundry, and even ironed his shirts. When she needed help, however, he was never available.

What Christy could not see was that she showed little regard for herself when she let him use her generous nature. He didn't even say "Thank you." She had no boundaries, so, of course, he took advantage of her. Most people tended to treat her the way she treated herself, which was not to hear or notice what Christy needed.

Christy acted like this as a way to be acceptable to others. I asked her, "What is it about yourself that you don't accept?" She replied, "If the people around me show any signs of not liking me, I fall apart. I start to obsess about it and can't think about anything else, except why they might not like me. I start remembering all the things I've done wrong and all the ways I've let people down, and it snowballs. I start to think I am the worst person in the world."

Christy had one or two friends she called frequently, seeking their comfort and validation, when her relationship began to fall apart. When she had these doubts and issues, however, she overdid it. She would stay on the phone for hours, complaining, analyzing, and going into detail about what he had said or done.

She was so needy and so out of touch with herself that it didn't occur to her that she was abusing her friends. She had no discernible limits as to what she would ask friends to do. Eventually, her friends stopped taking her calls. Christy was crossing their boundaries and taking advantage of their kindness. This caused her deep pain and confusion.

When she began to see that she had crossed the lines of others and demanding too much from them, she was appalled. It had never occurred to her that she had abused anyone. She perceived herself as a good and generous person. This new awareness shook her self-image.

Christy also came to realize that she liked being the problem solver and the caretaker for everyone, no matter what it cost her, because it made her feel important and needed. When this realization struck her, she paused and then said, "Perhaps thinking I was the 'only' person who could help my husband with his unhappiness, struggles, and wounded self-esteem was in fact, being arrogant." This epiphany almost knocked her down.

Pleasers are genuinely caring and loving people. However, they have not learned how to care for and love themselves first, so their noble intentions and nurturing qualities get convoluted, misguided, and misused. They have to guard against becoming enablers and keeping others from discovering their own truths and strengths.

These new insights were the beginning of setting new boundaries. When Christy had better boundaries, her in-laws and her own family members began to treat her better. She was no longer so desperate to please them.

Christy finally learned to focus her nurturing energy on herself. Instead of spending her time shopping and cooking for her husband, she began to work hard at learning new skills, looking for a job, and moving out of the marital house that no longer suited her needs.

Christy had a new Take: I will give myself the attention and kindness I seek. In doing this, I don't need the approval of others.

If you are suffering from people being unkind, unfair, and thoughtless toward you, take a good look at what you are allowing. You have to be clear, firm, and resolute about what works for you. You have to clearly define your external boundaries. And you have to be brave enough to risk losing some people in your life who don't treat you right.

Proactive Boundaries

Proactive boundaries are the measures you take to protect yourself *before* problems occur. Divorce is one of the most challenging situations you'll ever deal with. If you know that your ex's behavior is going to be trying, boundaries will help you take the necessary steps well in advance to avoid or lessen the fallout.

How can you tell when you need a proactive boundary? What are the signs to look for?

Does being around your ex drain you?

Does his family drain you? After being with them, do you feel tired or depressed?

Is your divorce experience exhausting?

Does your ex or someone in her family have to be the center of attention with her stories of what went wrong in your marriage?

Do you have some "friends" who always have to say something negative or mean that makes you feel bad about your breakup?

In situations such as these, you need to take proactive measures to protect yourself. If this feeling comes about every time you are with your ex, his family, or certain friends, you are forewarned of the imbalance they cause to your emotional equilibrium. It is your responsibility to prepare yourself. You need to gain some different strategies before you see them again.

For instance, you may find that if you take a good friend with you when you have to be with the drainer, your friend can help block some of the negative energy. You may decide to see the drainer in different settings, at different times—or even not at all. You have choices.

Maybe you have an ex who constantly breaks agreements, doesn't take ownership, or has irritating habits. How can you be proactive? This is what happened to Sharon.

Sharon's ex was *always* late, and this was just one of many issues that had caused their breakup. He arrived an hour behind schedule or didn't show up at all. It was never his fault. He lost his keys, his brother took his car, his mother needed groceries ... there was always a reason he couldn't make it. He also didn't bother to call her and let her know what was happening. And he never took personal responsibility for any of his tardiness.

Finally, one day as she sat waiting for him in the lawyer's office to discuss their property settlement, she knew she was being crazy. It was time for her to recognize that she was expecting something from him that he obviously couldn't give. She knew his pattern, yet she kept wanting and insisting that he be different. And when he wasn't different, she was irritated.

She was allowing his actions to upset her even though they were entirely predictable. The fact was—whether she liked it or not—he was always going to be late. From then on, if she wanted to see him about something important, she called him several times about the meeting they would have so that he wouldn't forget, and then she picked him up. She stopped being stressed about the way he was and took responsibility for what she had to do to finalize their divorce and communicate with him in the future.

Sharon's new Take: I accept people the way they are and don't expect them to be the way I want them to be.

Have you ever been in a relationship with someone who does the same things that hurt or irritate you over and over again? Do you keep expecting that person to be different? This is an example of when you need a proactive boundary. Think about what you are expecting before you are together so you can go into the situation prepared. Then get clear about what actions you will take to achieve a different result.

Responsive or Reactive Boundaries

Responsive or reactive boundaries are ones you put in place to remember that you don't have to take the bait when someone is argumentative, dismissive, insulting, or controlling. They help you maintain your dignity and keep you focused on the high road.

There are some situations you cannot avoid, like family get-togethers, reunions, visiting old friends, weddings, funerals, community events, recitals, and more. Someday the time may come when you have to go somewhere and you will be forced to see your ex or former in-laws. Some of them may be nasty, combative, or sarcastic.

These situations will try your patience. In some cases, your ex or those close to your ex will know the button to push to get you upset. Your sensitive issue could be anything from your weight to your job to your divorce. Reacting to the negative attitude only gives your ex more power—the very thing your ex wants.

Reactive boundaries prepare you for this, which is what my client Alice learned.

Alice was a successful executive vice president for a large corporation in a big city. Her husband was a poet and a part-time teacher. At forty-two, she had worked hard to achieve her prestigious position. Her father was especially proud of her, since he also worked in the corporate world. He had pushed, prodded, and coaxed her to the status and financial reward she now received.

Alice was the kind of person who put her heart and soul into everything she did. The problem was, at this point in her life, she felt empty—and trapped. She couldn't find any "soul" in what she was doing.

Married to a guy who counted on her to be the breadwinner and cowed by her father, she felt she had no other options. When I met Alice, I told her, "Remember this: you always have choices."

At first, Alice tried to talk to her husband about being unhappy in her work. He was incapable of seeing or hearing it. His social capital was in the reflected glory of his rich, brilliant wife. When she began to tell him that she wanted a different life, he made fun of her and told her she must be crazy. She found it impossible to talk to him without creating an argument that became ugly.

She went to her father and tried to talk to him. He got even angrier with her. Unfortunately, Alice's whole family was invested in her position; they all got a vicarious sense of importance from what she did.

After a few months of coaching, Alice had some idea of what she longed to do, even though she did not know how to stand up to her entire family and tell them she was going to do it. She wanted to enter a theological seminary. She wanted to become a minister and create a simple life. Naturally, she would make one-tenth of her current salary once she was finished with school and got a ministry.

Encouraged by the coaching process, Alice soon drafted a plan. She applied to schools, found some grants, and was ready to quit her job. She finally worked up the courage to tell her husband.

"*What?!*" he yelled. "You expect me to move and change my lifestyle? That isn't what I married you for!"

Alice set a boundary. She told him, "I can't go on living my life this way. Did you marry *me* or did you marry my success?" Cornered, Alice's husband confessed that he was not in love with her and would not stay married to her if she made this change, and he soon moved out.

Alice thought she would be devastated, but instead she felt enormous relief. She realized that she hadn't been happy with him, but instead had felt an obligation to take care of him. Once he left, she felt free.

Alice studied hard for the entrance exam and was accepted to a school that was perfect for her. When her plans solidified, she told her family.

Her father scolded her. "You gave up the job of a lifetime? What about your Harvard MBA? What about all the money you earn? You can't just throw all that away!"

Alice was emotionally ready for this reaction. She calmly replied, "I leave for school in a few weeks. I am very certain about my choice. I hope you will be happy for me. But if you're not, I understand. I love you."

Today Alice is a minister. She loves her work and the pace of her life. She told me she feels like she is on another planet. When she goes to visit her family, however, she sees that they are somehow embarrassed by her. They still introduce her to people as "the daughter with the MBA from Harvard." She takes it in stride.

Her ex has moved on. He has a new woman in his life who takes care of him. Alice is not bitter about what happened, even though she had to give him half of her savings in their divorce.

Alice's new Take is this: Living in the realm of great purpose is a blessing. When I live on purpose, the actions and attitudes of others don't cloud my decisions.

Alice told me that going through the divorce process was not so hard once she knew how to take care of her feelings and be prepared with her reactive boundaries.

The Challenge for Pleasers

Earlier in this chapter I told the story of my client Christy, a classic pleaser. Pleasers are nurturing by nature and often raised to believe that *always thinking of others first, before taking care of your needs, is a virtue.* My experience in working with clients has shown me that setting and maintaining boundaries can be a difficult hurdle for these people—but not impossible.

Pleasers do what they do because they feel it is just easier to go along with everyone else than to make waves. They can't stand confrontation, cannot bear for people to not like them, and think their job is to meet others' needs and "keep the peace."

Pleasers have an expectation when they are busy trying to meet everyone's needs. They are trying to get something from the people they are taking care of, but they don't speak up and say what they want. The problem is that they usually don't know what they want. They have forgotten their own needs for so long that they are out of touch with themselves.

How will you know you're a pleaser? How can you recognize when you are out of balance, giving more than you should, relenting when you don't want to, or supporting others when you haven't mastered finding support for yourself? Saying yes and going along with what others want, even when you feel you do not want to, will leave you with any of the following:

- A knot in your stomach
- A constriction in your throat
- An indefinable, gnawing anger
- Feeling like a disappointment because everyone's demands are more than you can possibly give
- A sense of being unappreciated
- Feeling hopeless, tired, and confused, and never understanding what people want
- Holding negative thoughts toward the person whom you allowed to cross your boundary

When you feel any of the above, you need to look at what boundary has been crossed. When you are in touch with how your boundaries work, it puts you in charge of how you are treated, how you feel, and what your appropriate reaction should be.

I often hear clients talk about things they didn't want to do but felt they had to, such as

- Going along with something their ex wanted because it seemed far easier than saying no
- Agreeing with their partner in order to keep the connection and feel appreciated

- Making their spouse and in-laws feel good—and if they don't feel good, it must be the fault of the pleaser
- Fulfilling the needs of the ex and both families so that the pleaser will feel important

You may also feel that to get your needs met, or to stand up for yourself, you have to get mad and tell people off. First of all, a true pleaser would have a hard time doing this. Second, you don't have to do this, except in extreme cases. It is possible to draw a line, not give in, and keep your cool. You can tell the offending party with kindness, humor, or metaphor that what he or she is doing doesn't work for you. Here is Kelly's boundary story.

Kelly was a full-time grad student, had a part-time job, and was married. She worked hard, she tried hard, and before coming to coaching, she was a pleaser. During her pleaser years, she did the housekeeping and rarely missed work. Her husband, Bobby, complained when he took the garbage out once a week. He was in law school and said that he didn't have time to help around the house.

Before Kelly knew about boundaries, she couldn't say no to anyone. This caused her relationship problems. She let people take advantage of her and didn't know how to stop them. Torn between doing a good job at work and school, being responsible for taking care of her home and her husband, and being a good person to her friends, she was always conflicted. Bobby was irritated with her and complained that she was never happy.

Kelly learned the necessity of boundaries when she agreed to go skiing with Bobby and his friends from school. She was tired and needed to study but felt guilty that she never had time to socialize. While they were out with his friends, Kelly noticed that Bobby was especially energized around one of his female classmates. They teased each other, made inside jokes that Kelly couldn't understand, and spent most of the day talking with each other.

Kelly was upset with him when they got home. He professed confusion and innocence around his relationship with his classmate and said he didn't know why Kelly was mad at him. He said that this other woman was simply his study mate. Suddenly, Kelly realized that she had been carrying the load for both of them while he was using his time to flirt with this woman.

When I met Kelly, she was feeling the pain and anger of betrayal. She said she no longer wanted to work and go to school full time and do everything else she had been doing. I told her that it sometimes takes a big jolt to wake us up to the reality that being a pleaser doesn't necessarily endear us to others or guarantee loyalty.

Kelly tried to get Bobby to go to counseling with her, but he refused. Finally, he confessed that he had been having an affair with his classmate and he was not going to give her up. The "old" Kelly would have stayed around, trying to win Bobby back, thinking she didn't deserve a man who could love her and be faithful. But the "new" Kelly asked him to leave. She did not yell or explode. She just knew that this partnership was over.

Kelly said that if Bobby wanted to go, she wanted him to go. She found a roommate, finished school, and began to use her new boundaries in all her friendships. She and Bobby are working out an amicable divorce.

Here is Kelly's new Take: I deserve to take loving care of myself. When I do, I am happier, make better choices, and have more energy to give to my priorities.

Visualize Your Boundaries

Setting boundaries takes practice, and one helpful way to do that is by imagining them already in place around you. Give it a try: When you are preparing for the divorce process

- Envision your boundaries, knowing they will protect you.
- Know that you will have the perfect response if someone is harsh or unkind. Feel yourself being safe.
- Begin to imagine an aura of light surrounding you as you stand behind your boundaries.
- Picture yourself in the setting: calm, in control of yourself, and handling any abrasive people who may be present or whom you used to dread being around.
- Visualize how you would like the event or the meeting to turn out for you. See how you're actually enjoying your new sense of control over your emotions.

If your ex begins to get you upset, consciously decide to respond appropriately, reminding yourself that this is not your problem. You are not a doormat, but you don't explode with anger either. You tell the truth, stay calm, and look to see how you can defuse the situation. The best thing to remember about responsive boundaries is that you are in charge of you. And isn't that a great feeling?

How to Strengthen Existing Boundaries

In order to have stronger boundaries, think about the following questions:

Do you allow your ex to make demands? Do you feel that you have to meet them? What boundary do you have now that you could strengthen?

What can you do in the next two weeks to let go of those old responsibilities you used to say yes to when you wanted to say no?

What part of your interaction with him feels out of control, and how can you make a stronger boundary work?

Can you think of ten things you will no longer allow your ex to do to you or say to you?

Have you been told by good, trusted friends that you make serious demands of your former partner? Think of the ways in which you might be crossing your ex's boundaries. Work on the ones you can start to eliminate.

How to Set New Boundaries

Now that you have an understanding of what boundaries are important for you, here are some examples of situations where you can recognize them and put them to action.

Interior boundaries: Your discomfort, in any form, is a signal to listen to yourself. Be kind to you. When you can do this, your ex and others will be more willing to treat you differently. You have to set the pattern for them.

Exterior boundaries: Your ex may want to bring you a crisis to solve. But remember that when you can't say no and when you make others' troubles your own, you aren't free to make good choices in other parts of your life. Choose to preserve yourself.

You will wear yourself out and not leave any time for the people who love you if you become caught up in your former partner's problems. Further, you will only be prolonging your ex's crisis if you listen and try to help. For example, notice that when he gets one problem solved, he finds ten more to take its place.

Proactive boundaries: Be clear about your limits with your ex. No one has the right to verbally, emotionally, or physically bully you. Good proactive boundaries are an antidote to bullying behavior. You can consider requests and make informed choices based on what you feel is worthwhile or necessary, but if he asks you to do something that makes you uncomfortable, you need to honor that feeling and not do it.

Understanding proactive boundaries also means avoiding some of the places where you know you will run into your ex. If you are going to dinner with friends, it is wise not to choose your shared favorite hangouts. Give the situation time to heal.

Responsive or reactive boundaries: When you set good boundaries, you will attract good people. If you keep a respectful distance from your ex's social life and avoid the people from your past who are difficult and draining, you will attract people who are strong, healthy, and accomplished. When you are going through a divorce, this is especially important.

But if and when you do come face-to-face with him or your former in-laws, even if they are distant, be gracious. If they are not warm or genuine, say a pleasant hello and step away from them so you don't get captured in a dialogue that will go nowhere.

The more care you give yourself and the more you stop others from leaping over your defined lines, the more you are available to whom and what you want.

Finally, this is how my client Andrea learned to set her boundaries and the rewards she reaped from doing so. Andrea was thirtysomething and wanted to meet a man and have a long-term relationship—possibly marriage. She had been married before, but because of her lack of boundaries, her husband and his family had intruded on every aspect of her life, often in cruel ways. When she could no longer take it, she left the marriage. When she came to see me, it became clear that she was one of the "nice people" who couldn't say no.

After years of being alone, she started to socialize. Her new boundary problem was that when she went out with friends to meet people, she invariably let some guy she was not interested in monopolize her evening. She didn't know how to excuse herself without thinking she was hurting his feelings. She couldn't gracefully walk away without guilt, so she never got the opportunity to meet someone else she might have liked.

She told me, "One night, I was caught in a conversation with a guy I didn't want to talk to for very long. But I couldn't get away from him. He kept talking and talking. Another very nice-looking man I was interested in kept walking by, looking at me like he was waiting to meet me. But the other guy never stopped talking. Finally, Mr. Attractive left. I was so frustrated!"

This is what a lack of boundaries will cost you. There is a way to talk to people, be kind, and move on. Andrea missed her chance, over and over, to meet someone she wanted to know while being "nice" to someone she didn't want to know.

After a few more of these evenings, she began to see what she was doing. She was wasting both her time and the time of the other person she was feeling sorry for. If she wasn't careful, this could become a repeat of settling for the wrong person.

One autumn day, Andrea went to a farmer's field to pick pumpkins with friends. She maintained a firm boundary with men who did not suit her, which freed up her time and attention that day and allowed her to focus her energy on attracting the right person. Her match did come along, of course. They dated for a year, got married, adopted a dog, bought a horse, and then had a baby. Andrea brought all this happiness into her life—through boundaries.

There is definitely a way to be elegant, dignified, and not defensive about stopping to say hello and then continuing to be social with others. You don't have to be apologetic. You can say, "It was nice talking to you," and then turn and walk in another direction. It is not okay to let someone rob you of your evening and your opportunities to explore other introductions. Once Andrea learned this, she was free to choose.

Boundaries will help you correct, re-craft, or develop anew your relationship with your ex, former in-laws, and everyone else. With your strong protective lines, you can handle anything. Start by embracing a different TAO:

• Your new Take: I have boundaries to protect me in any situation.

- Your new Actions: Knowing when, where, and how to enforce boundaries allows me to go where I need to and attend to what is important in my life.
- Your new Outcome: Feeling more confidence and calm and receiving positive responses from others give me optimism, hope, and clarity.

Now that you are equipped to build and enforce your boundaries, you are ready to enter the next stage along your TAO with a stronger sense of self. Throughout this section, you have been forming your Take as you have laid the groundwork for transformation, taken stock, and strengthened your boundaries. Have you noticed that former issues with your ex have diminished or even disappeared? Does your new Take leave you feeling confident, strong, and centered? In the next section, that Take will become the basis for your Actions, and you'll see that the time you invested in shaping a positive, fair, and authentic Take makes all the difference.

Suggestions for Building Boundaries in Relationships

What areas of your life are giving you problems? Where are you not listening to yourself? What changes can you make? Choose one to do this week.

Sit down with paper and pen and begin to write out what did not work for you in your past relationships. Look for the missing boundary that could have protected you.

Make a list of your ex's behavior patterns that caused you irritation. How can you draw a better boundary when you see him next?

What are your areas of sensitivity—"hot buttons"—that cause you to react negatively in situations when you feel pushed? How can you defuse this before you walk into it? What boundary do you need?

Make a list of the times your ex crossed a boundary with you. How could you have handled these differently?

Make a list of the times when you crossed a boundary with your ex. What would you do differently today?

Part II

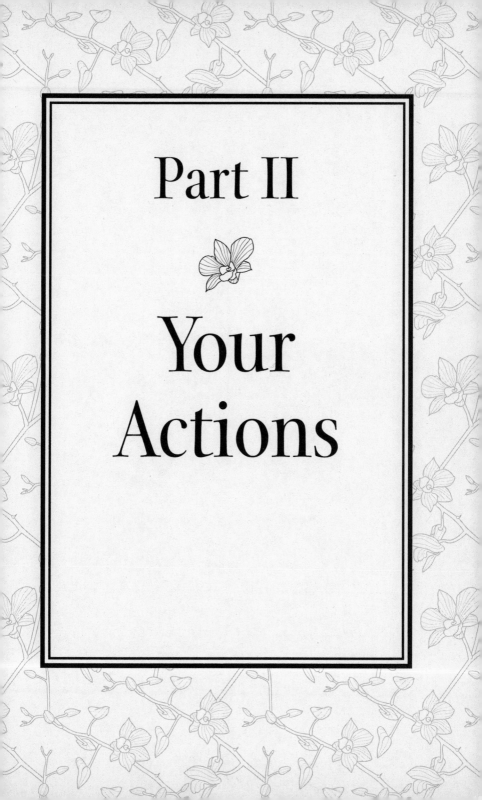

Your Actions

5
Cleaning House

The time that you have spent formulating your positive, constructive Take has prepared you for an important Action step: cleaning house. Just as you have let go of a marriage, which has left a vast space for possibility, it is also time to recognize and let go of what no longer serves you. Outdated habits, clutter, old emotions—whatever weighs on you, does not work for you, or interrupts your ability to embrace your new life—need to go. You must release your attachment to these burdens before you can freely progress along your new path— your TAO. You'll be amazed at how refreshing it feels.

Eliminating drainers gives you the energy and motivation to move forward. Drainers exist all around you in different forms and, without your realizing it, they sap your strength on a continuous basis. Whether from tiny leaks or huge gushers, you can lose your enthusiasm daily. That's why it's important to identify your drainers and do something about them now.

Physical clutter, things that no longer work, negative words, and emotional litter are your major drainers. You know it's a drainer when looking at it, listening to it, or thinking about it makes you tired. Eliminating drainers is essential because, underneath the rubble of your life, you will find you.

In this chapter, we'll identify the types of drainers you may be dealing with, both physical and emotional, and you'll learn how to clean them out of your life for good.

Clear the Clutter

We accumulate a lot of *stuff* during a marriage, and all that stuff has to be prioritized. What's important, what's worth keeping, what belongs to your ex, and what belongs to you? The stuff you keep requires a place, a purpose, and attention of one kind or another. If you don't need or have room for an item, or you have too many of the same thing, it becomes unnecessary clutter in your life.

What's wrong with clutter? It may seem benign, but it isn't. Whenever you have more material possessions than you need stacking up and cluttering your life, it's a burden.

Every time you look at it, you think about how you ought to do something with it. That thought is a distraction from your true purpose and focus: forming your new Take as you progress along your TAO. Every piece of clutter is like a tiny pinhole in your balloon of energy. If you get a lot of those little leaks, you will definitely go flat and then wonder why you're too tired to enjoy yourself. Clutter brings discouragement.

Physical de-cluttering starts with getting rid of what you have outgrown, what you no longer need, or what elicits unwanted memories. It is the physical action of doing something about the clutter that moves you into hope and possibility, as my client George found out.

George came to see me because he was terribly unhappy. His wife had recently left him after five years of marriage. Although he was nice looking, his clothes were wrinkled and he was slightly unkempt.

He said he was having a hard time coping and basically was falling apart. His mind was disorganized, which matched his even more disorganized apartment, he said.

When I work with clients, one of the agreements they make with me is to de-clutter some part of their living and working spaces every week. This activity makes them feel better almost instantly, which shifts their attitude and boosts their energy.

Being organized was not one of George's habits; he said his wife had handled that part of their lives. Each week he had an excuse for why he couldn't get started.

I suggested that he begin the process with just one drawer in his kitchen or the top of his desk. He said he'd try. At first, it seemed that he was just moving one pile of clutter from one side of the apartment to the other.

The problem was that his de-cluttering was irregular. He would do it for an hour one day and then not do it again for a week or two. I told George that building a new habit takes at least thirty days of consistent repetition. He needed to do something about his clutter every day.

After a few months, George showed up one day looking pretty spiffy, with his clothes pressed and his attitude more upbeat than before.

"Hey, George. What's happening?" I asked. "You look different."

"Do I? Yeah ... well ... I finally started cleaning up something every day. Yesterday, I washed the dishes and vacuumed, and then all of a sudden I really felt motivated! I started washing my sheets, taking my clothes off the chairs and hanging them up, and I'm amazed—things look good!"

"That's fantastic! I could tell that something big had happened the minute you walked in the door."

He smiled, which he had been doing more of lately, and said, "And also . . . I bumped into a woman who lives across the street from me, and she asked if I liked to ride bikes. I told her that I hadn't done it since I was a kid but that I'd like to get back into it. We made plans to go biking this weekend."

By continuing to make agreements with me about keeping his home and office de-cluttered, George managed to sustain his improved spaces and outlook. It wasn't long before I noticed that he no longer seemed lost without his ex-wife.

George's new Take: De-cluttering is energizing and leaves me feeling optimistic. His new Action: Taking care of his surroundings and making room for a new life.

My clients find it liberating to completely clean house following their breakup. The consequence of de-cluttering is the feeling of being in control of something. You can't do much to affect the grim daily news, wars and famine, or the suffering of others. And you can't control what is happening in your ex's life. You *can* control the quality of your own spaces, which miraculously affects your attitude and inner strength.

Have you ever experienced the rush of freedom that comes from cleaning your house deeply? Donna learned something about that after her breakup.

Donna did not have a contentious divorce. Her husband simply woke up one morning and said to her, "We are not in love anymore. I still care about you a great deal as a friend, but I am not 'in love' with you. I feel there is just more in life, yet I don't know what that 'more' is. I do know that I can't go on this way. I need to leave so I can find whatever it is that's out there for me."

Donna was numb and almost unable to speak. She knew he was right about the fact that they weren't in love, but she didn't think that it meant they had to end their marriage. She was quite comfortable in the life they had made together. Nothing was complicated, they rarely quarreled, and they had nice friends. Physical intimacy had stopped years ago, but that seemed a small loss compared to all they had.

Her husband told her, "You can have the house, your car, most of the furnishings, and half of our investments. I only want to take the things that were in my family. We can take turns sharing the beach house, but I will also put that in your name. Hopefully, you will leave it to the children in your will."

Donna knew there was no use in trying to argue with him. When he made up his mind about something, he was not going to budge. She had noticed that he had been growing more distant in the last few years, but she had not wanted to talk about it. She had been afraid that the truth would come out, which was that she didn't feel romantic toward him either.

Donna still saw her soon-to-be ex at the hospital where they both worked every day. It felt awkward. Was he dating? Was he in love? He seemed a lot happier, and the thought of him being with someone else drove her crazy. Whatever it was he wanted, why couldn't he have asked her for it?

They amicably shared their college-age children and even the housekeeper who had been with them since the children were born. Donna kept thinking he would change his mind and come back, but when the divorce was final, he said he was taking a few months off to go to India and study meditation. He didn't say whether anyone was going with him.

Donna could see that her ex was moving on, which made her feel miserable. When she was at home alone, she felt haunted by memories of the past. She told me that everything in the house reminded her of what was gone.

What could she do? I suggested that she could start with decluttering, reorganizing, and eliminating anything that made her feel sad. Pictures, mementoes, and gifts from the ex can sometimes be part of the emotional litter of the past. It all depends on what sort of attachment you feel when you look at various items.

She liked the idea of de-cluttering. She took a week off, hired some helpers, and took everything out of her house. She had everything scrubbed, painted, mended, and sorted. She put her stuff in three piles: Keep, Give Away, and Throw Away. She gave her ex and her children the things she didn't want to look at any-more. Pictures that were painful for her to see were boxed and put in the attic. Any object that gave her sad memories was dis-posed of or stored. In the process of this de-cluttering, as she touched objects and remembered where they had come from and the history they held, she found herself mourning and then let-ting go. She knew what parts of her past she wanted to keep and which ones she no longer wanted.

She reorganized her entire house. She bought a new bed and linens, rearranged the furniture, and eventually modernized her bathrooms and kitchen. Each project brought Donna another giant step into her new life. She was making her old house her new home.

Donna no longer brooded about what her ex was doing. Once her home was finished, she began to invite people over, have small dinner parties, and socialize with old and new friends. Not too long after that, someone fixed her up with a date. She couldn't believe she was dating.

When her ex returned from India, he announced that he was getting married. If Donna had not done her "work"—de-cluttering, creating a new home, and getting excited about her future—this was the kind of news that once would have flattened her. Instead, she was able to wish him well . . . and sincerely mean it.

What is Donna's new Take? My home is my comfort and spiritual oasis. Her new Action: My heart is big enough to wish the best for anyone.

What about your clutter? Do you know where most of it is? Here are some of the most prominent problem areas:

Closets

Clothes closets are probably the biggest challenge to de-clutter and the one area that will save you the most time when you pull it all together. Clothes need to be organized, arranged, clean, and easy to find. An unorganized closet can be a huge drainer when you are trying to find something to wear.

In addition, you may want to consider what clothing you want to recycle—items that hold unhappy memories for you. After a breakup, many people find that they want a different wardrobe for several reasons. Besides releasing negative or nostalgic thoughts the clothing reminds them of, some people want a fresh new image, with an updated wardrobe to reflect it.

Donating clothes from your old life can benefit the healing process. In addition to letting go of remembering past moments that evoke pain or regret, and feeling the optimism that comes from planning for your new image, you can feel good about knowing you are making a contribution to someone, somewhere, who needs them.

Since most of us have more than one closet that needs attention, start with de-cluttering the smallest one. Choose one day a week when you are going to spend an hour devoted to a closet. Notice the energy you feel when you finish cleaning out the first one. Then write on your calendar when you will do the next one. If you don't, you might not get to it.

Mail

Is your mailbox falling over, loaded with catalogs, magazines, advertising brochures, flyers, and envelopes of all sizes? Do you have a specific place to put everything when you bring it in?

Organize your mail into piles. Make an agreement with yourself: you will not let it accumulate for longer than one week. Immediately toss junk mail, and designate a drawer, cabinet, or office to hold items that will need attention later. You do not want to see your mail pile the minute you walk through the front door.

Drawers and Cabinets

The contents of drawers and cabinets are hidden when you close them, and as such they are "out of sight, out of mind"—until you need something and have to look for it. Give your batteries a huge recharge by sorting out all the stuff that has accumulated in those easy-to-forget places. Again, tackle one area at a time.

Countertops, Tables, Desktops

Clutter on countertops and other surfaces is the clutter you see when you walk through the door. It makes you feel weary. You may think you are immune to how much it bothers you, but it enters your field of energy nonetheless. I know people who have not been able to eat at their kitchen or dining room table in years because they have so much stuff on top of it. If clearing these spaces feels like an overwhelming job that you can't think about, put all the clutter in stacks and then take it down and deal with it, one piece at a time.

Hidden Spaces

You may have an attic, garage, shed, trunk, or tucked-away space that other people don't see but you know is there. It lurks in the back of your conscious or subconscious mind. If you find yourself procrastinating, ask a friend or hire a high school student to help you clean it out.

When all your spaces are handled, you will feel more powerful than a superhero. Who knew you could just flip a switch and turn on your energy by resolving that you will clean up the clutter? In the process, you will have made room for the people you love, as well as the new friends you are about to make. You will have the space to engage in your hobbies and interests. And most of all, you will have prepared a special place that can welcome calm, peace, and your continually growing spirit.

Stop Tolerating What's Not Working

What are you putting up with? Whether you are at home or at work, there is probably something broken, stained, torn, or just plain not working. You look at it and think, "I've got to handle that one of these days." But you keep putting it off, finding that you never get to it. It may seem too insignificant to take up your time.

If you understood that this is another way you leak energy, you would place it higher on your list of priorities. The truth is that every time you see it, it brings up feelings of guilt, hopelessness, or irritation, and those feelings drain you.

Discussing tolerance one day with a long-distance client, I asked her, "So, what have you been tolerating in your life? It might have been there for so long that you've gotten used to it and you don't quite 'see' it anymore. But you probably notice it when someone new walks in the room, and when you do, it grates on you."

"Interesting you should mention that," she said. "As we talk each week, I sit here looking at the broken light fixture hanging over the dining room table. My husband had always told me he was going to fix it. Then he left, with no warning. It's been broken for years. Every time I look at it, I get mad."

She went on to explain, "My ex and I are on civil terms with each other. But there's something about that broken light I guess I've wanted to hang on to. It reminds me of how he never kept his word or did what he'd said he would. Keeping it there has reminded me of why we never got along and it's made it easier to let him go.

"I think I've tolerated it long enough." She laughed. "I'm ready to get rid of the fixture *and* the anger."

The light fixture she had been tolerating was the tip of the iceberg for my client. She went on to find other things that needed fixing, and when she got them under control she became more hopeful and her life more vibrant. She realized that they had kept her stuck in her negative feelings for her ex and that she could fix these things herself, as well as handle her own life, without needing to blame someone else for any of it not working.

Her new Action was to take care of what she was tolerating, which left her free of negativity.

What are you tolerating in your space? Take a walk around your home and do an inventory. They could be there even though you just don't notice them anymore. And make no mistake: they're still drainers. Here are some examples:

- Burned out lightbulbs
- Spots on the carpet or the furniture
- Junk in your car or in the trunk of your car
- Broken chairs, tables, dishes, or appliances
- Walls, trim, or decks that need paint
- Peeling wallpaper that needs to be removed and changed
- Broken doorknobs, handles, faucets, or other hardware
- Weeds in the yard, shrubs that need trimming, or dead plants in your house
- Pictures on the floor that you plan to hang someday
- Doors or cabinets that stick when you try to open them
- Broken switches, cords, or shades
- Torn cushions
- A garage so full of stuff that you can't park your car in it

Start with these questions: what am I putting up with that I no longer want to tolerate, and what do I need to do about it? Get started now, and you'll feel a huge burden lifted.

Notice Your Words

Words have unlimited power—for good and bad—in your life. When you speak negatively, you drain your own hope, optimism, and excitement.

Since your words become your Actions, it is imperative that you *listen* to what you say. You may be mindlessly repeating what you have heard others say—from your friends to even certain television characters—and be unaware of what you are literally speaking into your reality. You could be developing a negative Take without realizing it, unconscious of how it is shaping your life.

In other words, what you say can become fact. The divorce process can play havoc with your self-esteem, so pay attention to the following expressions, or others like them, and eliminate them from your self-talk or daily conversations with others.

I'll never get through this alive.

This divorce is killing me.

I'll never love anyone again.

If I ever meet another guy, he'll probably cheat on me too.

I've given the best years of my life to the wrong woman.

I'll never trust myself in another relationship.

I'm damaged goods, and no one good would ever want me.

These negative statements can invoke unwanted feelings, actions, reactions, and beliefs, for you and your future. If this is what you are putting out there, this is what you are going to get back. This is how the TAO works: your words and thoughts lead to your actions, which bring you the Outcome you want. These words may come from your fears, self-criticism, or the impossible standard you hold yourself to. Whatever the reasons, you can choose not to entertain these negative words in any form.

Take responsibility for the nasty dust you can stir up in your psyche when you utter certain words. They may seem harmless; you may think you are just joking; it might seem that if no one can hear them, it doesn't matter. But it does matter because you can hear them, as does your subconscious mind, which creates your future.

The story of Will and Faye is like one I have heard countless times from people who have had the same experience. Will and Faye went to their twenty-fifth high school reunion and met up again. Besides going to the same high school, they had attended colleges that were close to each other. They had always been good friends but had never dated.

After college, Faye took a job in another state. When she went home to visit her parents, she inquired about Will. She also knew what he was doing through mutual friends and family, but she didn't see him again.

Will said he had never forgotten her. He knew he was in love with her but thought she was so beautiful and talented that she would never be interested in him. Faye dated some of his friends in college, and he often saw her at football games and college parties. When she moved away, Will often visited her brother and knew about Faye's life through him.

Faye said she had never known that Will liked her. She said he was always fixing her up with one of his friends, and she took that gesture to mean that he wasn't interested. She thought he was too handsome and wonderful to ever be attracted to someone like her.

Faye got married when she was thirty. When Will got an invitation to her wedding, he knew his chances with her were over. He didn't go because he couldn't bear to watch her marry someone else. He got married two years later.

When Faye and Will saw each other at their reunion, they were both divorced. She was thrilled to see him again. After talking through the night, Will finally told her that he had been in love with her his whole life. She was stunned. It had never occurred to her that he felt that way.

This is what happens when you tell yourself you aren't good enough and that you don't deserve or can't have who or what you want. You believe your words and live your life from them.

Will and Faye are working through the process of mourning the years they lost from being apart. They are also planning a new future, trying to adjust to being so happy.

Have you had your words become true after speaking them? Have you ever spoken negatively of yourself or someone else and then felt limp afterward? Did you wonder why? Whenever dismissive, critical, cynical, sarcastic, or negative predictions escape from your lips, they are drainers, and you are leaking energy. Replace them with positive words and you will feel restored.

Clean Up Emotional Litter

There's another kind of clutter in your life, but it's easy to miss because it isn't necessarily tangible. I call it emotional litter. It's more insidious than other kinds of clutter, eating away at your ability to create your dreams and desires.

Emotional litter comes in all sizes. Essentially, it is the negative people, baggage from the past, anger, hopelessness, guilt from your divorce, and anything else that occupies your emotional land-scape. If you find yourself in the middle of it, remembering it, or listening to it, and it makes you feel bad, it's time to clean it up.

You may have noticed how certain people or places affect you. Empower yourself by knowing that you will start to identify what drains you and use that awareness for self-protection. Some people use the term "energy vampires" to describe people who drain them.

My client Abby told me that she had a nosy next-door neighbor who often asked her how she was doing and how her husband was doing. Eventually, the questions became more than polite neighborly talk. This neighbor wanted to know what time he came home or where he was. She insinuated that she knew about their marital problems and bullied Abby to tell her more.

After talking to her neighbor, Abby felt weak, worthless, and emotionally out of control. The woman's tone and attitude were accusing and her questions prying. Abby felt that the woman was like a huge hungry vulture pecking her apart. Since Abby didn't know how to set good boundaries, soon she was hiding in her house, afraid to go out for fear she would have to face another inquisition.

Abby didn't have just an energy leak—she had a gusher! These exchanges with her neighbor were power outages that took hours and days to recover from. Abby was already depleted from trying to deal with a husband who would not say whom he was spending time with and why he didn't come home on some nights.

Abby did not start to feel like she would make it through the divorce until she learned to set boundaries with Ms. Pecking Vul-ture. Once Abby handled her, she was strong enough to let go of a marriage that was not really there anymore.

Abby's new Take: I will take loving care of myself by not allowing anyone to bully me. Her new Action: Choosing not to engage in unwanted dialogue or questions. This made her feel empowered.

The sour attitude of anyone who makes comments or asks questions that upset you can cause energy leaks. Set new boundaries with toxic people or let them go. This will make room for the new people you do want in your life—people who have warmth and aliveness. When you have positive, creative, imaginative people around, their energy is infectious.

Likewise, certain memories can make you feel uncomfortable whenever you think about them. If this is the case for you, look to see how you can mend a relationship, reframe the memory, or repair yourself. Ask yourself these questions:

Do you need to apologize to someone face-to-face?

Do you need to forgive yourself for letting someone intimidate, bully, or harass you in any way? How would you handle that person differently today?

Do you want to write a letter to someone you once had a bad relationship with and get your feelings and thoughts out on paper? You can do this and not mail it if sending it to the person would make the situation worse.

Did the person who is the source of your bad memories pass away, and it is too late to make amends? Pretend the person is alive, sitting in a chair in front of you, and tell him or her every-thing you wish you could have said before the chance passed.

Do you have incomplete communications with anyone in your life that hold you back from the relationship of your dreams?

Memories laden with angst are the emotional litter you don't need. Forgive the person, forgive yourself, and move on.

Most of us, especially when coming out of a relationship, have an accumulation of clutter, litter, and things we are tolerating. My own experience of cleaning house after divorce was a breath of fresh air. I had never gone through and sorted out the stuff acquired over the years.

There was an exhilarating freedom that came from being organized. It gave me the clarity to see that there was a deeper cleaning I needed to do. Finally, I had the strength not only to see it but also to do it.

Like a recovering addict, I needed to make amends. I had tried to put a happy face on an unhappy life, and I had stretched the understanding of friends and family. After I apologized for the discomfort I'd brought them, we had a new connection and bond.

Discovering the *power* of cleaning up relationships gave me confidence, hope, and a great release. I wasn't aware of how I had carried past regrets inside, how much they weighed on my heart, and how they validated my negative opinion of myself, affecting my decisions.

At this point in your TAO, study what you are living with, decide what is draining you, and make a plan to clean house. When you feel the power you have earned by eliminating your drainers, you will be able to focus your energy on the people, activities, and dreams that really sustain you.

Here are some suggestions to try out for eliminating emotional drainers:

Word watch. Monitor your own words. Do not fall into the unconscious habit of using slogans or clichés if they are negative in any way. Every time you hear yourself state a limiting thought, use edgy words or condemn others or yourself, write it down, tear it up, and throw it in the trash. That's where it belongs.

Clutter clusters. Identify the areas you need to de-clutter and write the date of when you will do it in your notebook or journal. Make your own list if this one isn't detailed enough.

- Closets
- Cabinets
- Drawers
- Desks
- Counters
- Tabletops
- Rooms
- Attic
- Garage

Troublesome tolerance. Make a list of what you tolerate in your home and work space. Do you have any of the following on this list? How will you get them handled and when will you do it? Assign a date to each item.

- Stains
- Broken objects
- Torn objects
- Items that need painting

- Items that need scrubbing
- Appliances that need repair
- Furniture that needs repair

Negative people, situations, and events that make you tired. Go back and read about boundaries in chapter 4. Where do you need a better boundary? When do you feel emotionally weak? Who is there when it happens? What is going on?

Make a list of all the places and people that drain you. Strategize a plan to either eliminate these drainers or shift your approach in dealing with them.

6
Getting into Alignment

Living in alignment means that your thoughts, words, feelings and actions are in support of the future you desire and you are living your life honoring your values. Nothing can hold you back from the new vision you have for yourself. Being in alignment makes you feel whole, brings you more of what matters most, and provides the opportunity to be in a better relationship with your ex.

Being in sync is a glorious feeling. When your actions match your words and thoughts, all parts of you are pulling in the same direction. Being out of alignment can make you miserable. No one intentionally gets out of balance, but it happens.

Before I understood alignment, I often found myself in situations like this: An old boyfriend of mine, who was an outdoor jock, was invited to join several couples at the beach . . . and bring me. Since I was no jock, every adventure he'd planned as a surprise turned into a nightmare for me and, therefore, for him too. This particular day started with waterskiing on the choppy bay. Since I'm not a skier or long-distance swimmer, this was frightening. Instead of declining, however, I slipped out of the boat and into frigid waters and into the skis. The boat took off, pulling me around and around for what seemed like hours. I waved to him

97

and his friends to stop but they just waved back, thinking I was having a good time.

Unfortunately, that was just the beginning. Being a "pleaser," I didn't speak up as we headed to a cove to dive for fish, which they caught and ate for lunch. My appetite was zero; I was seasick from riding the waves. They were having a great time while I hoped they didn't notice my lack of participation. I was just trying to survive. We headed off to another beach for an afternoon of volleyball.

Finally, dark settled over the beach as I watched the last game from the sidelines. Hair full of sand, gritty all over, in sticky icky clothes, and after ten hours in the sun, I thought, *Surely it's time to leave.* But it wasn't. We moved on to one couple's apartment. Covered with sand, some people drank beer and cooked hot dogs while a few of us listened to loud music, shouting across the room to each other in "conversation." I forced a smile, did my best to get through it, and fought with the boyfriend all the way home.

I was obviously out of alignment that day. My thoughts, feelings, actions, and words did not match up. I said I was having a good time when clearly I wasn't. Every part of me, from my head to my toes, was full of sand . . . and out of sync.

Ultimately, the boyfriend and I broke up. My lack of alignment was not just in the activities I didn't want to do with him. Relationships usually don't break up over divergent interests. They fall apart over something much more relevant.

The truth was that he was not what I wanted him to be, nor was I the person he would have preferred. I realized that I was blaming him for my lack of alignment when the only one who could make that inner shift was myself. If I had been even remotely in touch with myself, I would not have been there . . . because I wouldn't have been in the relationship.

If you find yourself somewhere not having a good time, stop and assess your alignment. Your unhappiness has nothing to do with those around you or the activities you're engaged in or anything else except your own *personal choices* and, unfortunately, how you have betrayed yourself. Think of unhappiness as a key indicator that you are out of alignment—and then take steps to fix it.

We come together in relationships to learn from each other and grow. Breaking up is a time to look and see what was not working for you, where your illusions collided with the reality of the situation, and what the signs were that you didn't want to notice from the beginning. All of this is rich with opportunity for your own deeper awareness, but you can't take advantage of it if you are stuck in thinking that your unhappiness was someone else's fault.

The Downside of Faking Alignment

Why do people stay together when they are out of alignment? Many of my clients say they stayed in a bad relationship for years because they were afraid: afraid to be alone, afraid they couldn't make enough money to take care of themselves, or afraid of what their families would say if they got a divorce. Their thoughts and feelings were not about love but *pretend love.* Therefore, their lives were tangled and incongruent.

I heard an old joke once that described one of the many reasons why people stay married. A man and woman in their nineties went before a judge at the local courthouse to get their final decree of divorce. The judge, peering over the bench, was astonished when he saw them. He groped for words, scratched his head, and finally said, "Tell me, why would two people who have been together for as long as you have get a divorce at your age?"

"Well," the man said, "we had to wait for all the kids to die. We didn't want to upset them."

If you stay in a marriage for financial security, like many people do, there will always be a price to pay. When you tell someone you love him in order to keep him around, even when most of the time you don't even *like* him, you are going to be irritable. When you are allowing someone else to take care of you while you stay away from economic responsibility, you also may be angry, guilty, depressed, accusing, and blaming your partner for your misery.

You can fake alignment for a while, but the results never serve you in the end, as my client Margo found out.

Margo was an artist and budding actress from New York when she met a cowboy while doing summer stock in Arizona. She was thirty-two and he was thirty-five. They had been married for three years when he left her for another woman.

"When I first met him," she said, "he fulfilled all my fantasies of being swept off my feet and literally being carried away by Prince Charming on a white horse—actually, it was a golden Palomino. I thought it was so romantic!"

Margo explained that being a free spirit and an artist, she had never had enough money to live on and had had to borrow from friends and family. Her cowboy was lonely, had never met anyone like her, and was eager to take care of her. They married two months after they'd met.

Margo said, "I was never 'in love' with him, but when I first met him, I thought he was sweet."

She continued, "I did my best to settle down in the community. I taught an acting class at the local Y and got some parts in summer theater. But basically, I missed New York and the pace of life there, and I was bored. We began to fight.

"I started to notice the things he did that drove me crazy. His idea of getting dressed up was a pair of clean jeans, a short-sleeve shirt, and his nicer pair of boots. Other things that made me nuts were that we never went anywhere elegant, we had nothing to talk about, and I was never going to stop being afraid of horses."

I said, "I understand that some of his ways were hard for you to appreciate, but what do you think the real issue was?"

She thought for a minute and then said, "I was never physically attracted to him. Shortly into the marriage, I noticed that I didn't like the way he smelled, talked, dressed, or ate his food."

"So what were your reasons for being there?" I asked her.

"The truth is," she said, "I didn't know how to take care of myself. I stayed in the marriage for financial security."

"What were the things you told your husband?"

"I told him that I loved him ... I was basically acting ... but I also worked at trying to change him so that he wouldn't irritate me so much."

"Did you complain about him to his face or behind his back?" I asked.

Unfortunately, she had done both, which only caused Margo to feel more guilty and trapped, with her husband growing more distant.

I asked, "What did you gain and what did you lose when you struck this bargain of marriage?"

"I definitely found a way to have enough money to live, but I lost my freedom," she said.

"What else did you lose?" I asked.

"I don't know. My life in New York?"

"I suspect it was bigger than that," I said. "How did you feel when you told him you loved him but you didn't mean it?"

"I felt terrible. But I wasn't doing anything thousands of other women don't do every day to survive," she said.

"I'm not coaching thousands of women right now," I said. "I'm coaching you. And we're trying to get you to a place where you can feel whole and fulfilled. But that's not possible when your thoughts, feelings, and words don't match up."

"Yeah, but he betrayed me!" Margo blurted, tears starting to form. "He had an affair with another woman and asked me to leave."

"How did you first betray *yourself?*" I asked.

"I get it," she nodded. "I was betraying myself and him when we married, because I knew I didn't love him. When he figured that out, he found someone else."

Margo had felt that *she* was the injured party when she got her divorce. Because he had been unfaithful, she could easily shift the blame to him for the marriage not working. Until she came to coaching, she thought that everything wrong in the relationship was his fault.

The truth was, they were both out of alignment. He had been lonely, desperate to marry anyone, without realizing he needed someone who shared his values. Initially, he loved her theatrical antics, but once they were married, they wore thin. He thought she would settle down, become appreciative of him, and act like a "grown-up."

Margo was totally out of balance, being with a man strictly for financial reasons. Looking for someone to pay her bills, she didn't stop and consider who she was really marrying and whether the life she had bartered for would work for her.

Margo began to get her life in order. She could see how her feelings, actions, thoughts, and words had never matched up when she was in the marriage. She understood what she had done.

She wrote her ex a long letter and apologized. He called her, and though he was a little distant, he thanked her for the letter and apologized too. She realized that he had always been a nice man and still was. They send each other a Christmas card each year with a note about how they are doing.

Margo is now focused on this Action: She takes responsibility for her life first, before making important decisions.

Blaming the other person entirely for the failure of the relationship is common, especially when you want that person to be someone different from the person you married. Can you see that when you put yourself in a place where you don't want to be, expect people to act the way you want them to, and then fight with them to change, there is no end to how far off track you can get?

Putting your life in alignment can solve many unnecessary problems. When your internal system is in sync, you will be much less likely to make poor decisions, become the victim in relationships, or engage in blaming other people for your unhappiness. When you are in alignment, you are comfortable with yourself and everyone else. Alignment brings you an enormous freedom in allowing people to be just the way they are.

Aligning with Reality

Another common alignment problem that occurs in breakups is when one person is still in love with the ex. People in this situation may be *acting* like a friend to the ex, trying to stay connected to his or her life. But acting one way and feeling another is deception, and that will always bring problems, misunderstandings, and false hope. Instead of fooling yourself, it's time to align with reality and accept the situation.

One of my clients, Maureen, couldn't get over her ex. She had met Troy, a dashing forty-two-year-old professor, when she went to a history conference at her former university. He had never been married and was immediately smitten with her.

Forty-five-year-old Maureen was coming out of a long, painful marriage and had three children, an elderly mother, five dogs, two cats, and a canary. She was a high school history teacher.

Troy fell madly in love with Maureen and rushed her for an exclusive commitment. Confused, she said no ... and then she said yes. But just as quickly as he'd met her and descended upon her life, he left to pursue another job and a much younger woman in another state. Maureen was devastated and confused. She thought she had met her soul mate.

What Maureen did not understand at the time was that his behavior was a red flag of danger. This "I-love-you-but-don't-count-on-me" pattern was bound to show up again. Unfortunately, he returned a year later, begging forgiveness and offering marriage. She said yes.

Maureen spent twelve years married to Troy. He betrayed her with other women, would not show up when she needed his emotional support, kept his own apartment and only spent the weekends with her, and ran up her credit card debt. Broken-hearted, she divorced him.

"Where were you out of alignment?" I asked her.

"From the very beginning," she said, "I knew not to trust him. But when we were together, it was so fabulous. We could talk and have fun, and we were very attracted to each other."

"What else did you know about him?" I asked.

"He never showed up for his parents or his friends when they were in need," she said. "He resented my mother and my children. He never did anything to help me take care of my responsibilities. In fact, he wanted me to abandon them, which I would never do. That's why I divorced him. But why do I still love him? I keep waiting for him to change and come back and be happy with me. When it was good, it was so good."

I said, "When you are not taking exquisite care of yourself, giving yourself what you need, you are vulnerable to someone who acts the way you want him to. Abusive, selfish men who look for women they can use can be charming . . . but cunning. They know what you want to hear. If you are not living a life you *treasure*, you will give your power away to them because the promise of what they offer seems so much better than what you have going on for yourself."

I continued, "To be in alignment, you have to shift your belief that you don't deserve anything, reframe your negative thoughts and words about yourself, and develop strong boundaries. If you stop being the perpetual pleaser, you will have the ability to see and hear the danger signals—and the strength to *choose* to walk away from any existing chemistry. This is called taking care of yourself. Just because something looks good and feels good doesn't mean that it is good. You deserve more than crumbs. You deserve a banquet!

"When you think about being alone, what are your thoughts? Do you think you are too old to find love? Does it seem impossible to go out there and find your real soul mate? Do you believe that there really aren't any good men left in the world, and if there were, that they wouldn't want you? These are all lies, and if you value the truth, you will work these phrases out of your brain.

"Do you see how these thoughts are not in alignment with self-love? Self-love is imperative before you can have an equal exchange of love with another."

Maureen is working on shifting her negative Take on relationships, monitoring her self-defeating thoughts, and letting go of her ex. She is getting involved in energy-producing activities like de-cluttering and exercise. She wants to get in shape and start dating.

Maureen said she is not ready to be close friends with her ex. She doesn't want to fall back into asking him to come home. She says she looks forward to the day when she can be around him and not feel an emotional tug. Maybe then they can talk as friends.

Maureen's new Take: I am creating a gorgeous new life. Her new Action is that she no longer clings to the past or her ex.

When it is difficult for one person in a relationship to let go, it is usually a sign of reluctance to grow. She wants to hang on to the way she *wanted* it to be, she wants the *illusion* of a relationship, and, most of all, she can't believe that it is possible to create a different, better, happier life. Once she aligns with reality, she is fully able to let go and embrace what her new life holds.

By Aligning, You Avoid Mistakes Before They Happen

Here is another story of someone who fell out of alignment when she met the wrong guy. She felt her biological clock ticking and was desperate to have a home and family. That motivation was so powerful that she lost her way.

Shelly, a thirty-nine-year-old divorced woman, was looking for a relationship. She had no children from her first marriage and was anxious to start a family.

Shelly met a man, was mildly attracted to him, and eventually let him move in with her. She then asked him to leave several times but relented and let him stay. She felt that time was running out for her and wanted to believe he could be the one. But in her quiet moments, she knew she wasn't in love with him. She was depressed.

Shelly came to see me because she wanted reassurance that maybe they could work it out. She wanted some magic "tips" to help her change the guy and change the relationship so they could get married.

"Do you like this guy?" I asked.

"Sometimes. He's not so bad. He can be really sweet. Most of the time, though, I'm not too sure. He only works on and off, and he doesn't try very hard at getting a full-time job. I'm paying all the bills right now."

"Do you tell him you love him, even when you don't feel it?"

"Yeah."

"What would you say are some of your most important values?" I asked.

"Being a good person," she said.

"What is a good person? What makes people good?"

"Being nice to others. Being honest. Being fair," she answered.

"Do you think you are an honest and fair person?" I asked.

"Yes. Most of the time."

"If you are not honoring your core values, that is a source of your depression," I explained. "Let's look at those values. Being a 'nice' person is important to you. If you are not in love with this guy but you tell him you are, is that 'nice'? Is it fair? And is it honest? When you're not thinking and feeling what you say, you're out of alignment with yourself."

Shelly was torn between her need to settle down and have children and the fact that the man she was with was not someone she loved . . . or liked.

107

Shelly asked her boyfriend to move out within a few days. She told him she did not have the kind of feelings for him that hold couples together.

After he left, Shelly felt a great sense of relief and freedom. She was back in sync with herself and no longer upset with him for all the things he couldn't be. They aren't close friends, but when they see each other, they are very kind.

Self-discovery, valuing who she is, and finding out what her requirements are for a relationship are Shelly's new goals.

Shelly's new Take: My deepest value is honesty. Shelly's new Action: She always tells herself the truth.

When you are saying one thing, thinking another, feeling something else, and taking actions that are contrary to all the above, you are in pieces. You will have an impossible time finding inner strength and harmony.

Identifying Core Values

Here is a valuable way to discover how to be aligned: identify your core values so you can recognize when you are not living from them. For instance, if you value truth but you meet someone who is an obvious liar and you go out with the person anyway, you are betraying the deepest part of yourself. When you know the person isn't honest *and* you are trying to ignore that fact—which is deceiving yourself—you will be in constant conflict. You will doubt yourself, you will try to change the person, and ultimately, if you stay together, you will feel all your dreams vanish because your energy is channeled into survival.

Core values are central to the meaning of your life. They are the standards and principles that are at the center of your being. They resonate with your heart and your soul. When you act in line with these highest values, you have integrity. This is the way you develop and maintain self-esteem. Living from these values brings you alignment.

If you are not connected or aligned with your values, it can lead to depression, insecurity, and a lack of fulfillment. People can often be despondent and not understand why. Instead of finding the way to their inner harmony, they look to other people, relationships, or marriage to make them whole. And then they are disappointed when they don't feel any better.

Here are some of the situations and signs that will indicate you are out of alignment:

Are you depressed after being with two people who are obviously in love with each other? This depression is an alignment alert. Ask yourself what you have done lately to give love to yourself. Are you thinking good thoughts about yourself, speaking kind words, meeting with close friends, doing your favorite hobbies, and feeding your soul?

Were you angry when someone made a mean judgment about you? Were you silent, or did you speak up with kindness, letting the person know that you don't feel appreciated when you hear those words? To alleviate the anger, check out your own silently held judgments about yourself and others. If any of them are unkind, reframe them into positive, affirming statements.

Have you ever felt that you couldn't trust someone but didn't pay attention to your inner knowing? Eventually, did that person do something untrustworthy? Learning to heed your inner

alarms comes from trusting yourself. What other circumstances have you been in where you did not trust
your wisdom?

Here is an example of how one person discovered a core value,
which became the deal breaker for his relationship. Andy is a
divorced man who found a woman he thought might be his future
wife. But sometimes he had some uneasy feelings about her.

He came to see me because he was getting more upset each
day as he struggled to identify what it was. His doubts and wor-
ries confused him, he thought he was being a bad person to have
them, and he blamed himself for thinking that this was just his
way of getting "cold feet" and not marrying her.

He said, "My girlfriend is kind, attentive, beautiful, and well
educated. We go to church together, hike in the mountains, love
each other's dogs, and talk about the future. I don't know what's
the matter with me and why I doubt her. Everyone tells me how
lucky I am that I've found her."

I asked, "Have you ever seen her do something that was out
of alignment? For instance, does she say hello to someone, chat
him up, fawn over him ... and when he is out of sight tell you
how she hates him?"

"Well," he said. "It seems like she has this 'nicey-nicey' behavior with me. It doesn't feel real, but maybe I'm reading it wrong."

Before his next session, Andy got the answer to his nagging
doubt.

Early one morning in the middle of the week, he stopped by
his girlfriend's house to drop off a surprise gift on his way to work.
He saw her car in the driveway and quietly let himself in with his
key so he wouldn't wake her. She didn't hear him enter as she sat
in her living room watching TV—with another man. They were
both in their robes.

Andy's deepest values were fidelity and trust. Why couldn't he pick up the clues that something was not right from the beginning?

When you are focused on marriage and family; when the chemistry is fantastic; when you've met her parents and she's met yours and everyone seems happy; and when someone is beautiful, successful, and paying a lot of attention to you, you don't want to notice the first, second, and third time you have troubling thoughts that something is wrong.

Andy's new purpose in life is to remember his core values and use them to get aligned.

Currently, Andy is dating new people. He said that he does not want to be friends with his ex—or anyone else he can't trust.

What is Andy's new Take? I will trust my inner voice and not dismiss it. Andy's new Action: He goes slowly in new relationships.

What Matters to You?

Read the following list. Then choose five to ten of the following qualities that resonate strongly with you. In order to identify what is essential in your life, use this phrase as a tool to help you find the values that matter most.

It is *most* important to be:

accepting	athletic	caring
accomplished	authentic	child oriented
addiction free	balanced	classy
admirable	beautiful	committed
adventurous	bold	communicative
affectionate	brilliant	compassionate
artistic	calm	competent

continued on next page

continued from previous page

confident	generous	playful
content	handsome	predictable
cooperative	happy	prosperous
creative	hardworking	quiet
cultured	healthy	religious
curious	home oriented	respectful
debt free	honest	responsible
decisive	humble	rhythmical
dependable	independent	secure
disciplined	influential	sexy
diversity oriented	intelligent	social
educated	joyful	spiritual
elegant	kind	spontaneous
emotionally aware	listening	stable
ethical	loving	strong
exciting	loyal	structured
fair	masculine	successful
faithful	moderate	supportive
family oriented	musical	tolerant
feminine	natural	traditional
financially secure	nurturing	trustworthy
flexible	open-minded	truthful
forgiving	outgoing	wealthy
friendly	passionate	wholesome
frugal	patient	willing
fun loving	peaceful	wise
funny	pet oriented	witty

When you are connected to your values and when your words, thoughts, feelings, and actions are all working in concert, this is alignment. Nothing can pull you off track. No one can tempt you, distract you, intimidate you, or even confuse you. You are spiritually in the flow, taking the action and making the contribution you were sent here to make.

Here are some suggestions to find self-alignment:

Words, thoughts, feelings, and actions

Write down some of the times in the past when you were out of alignment in words, thoughts, feelings, or actions.

What were you doing?

What were you trying to achieve?

Is there anyone you want to apologize to?

What do you need to forgive yourself for?

Values

Review the list of values on pages 111–112. Use the following sentence to help you gain deeper clarity about the qualities that are important to you. To complete this sentence, write down the five values that you think are absolutely necessary for a good life.

I would not be happy with myself if I was not

_____

_____.

Self-esteem

Using the list of values again, answer the questions on the next page:

Which qualities on the list are you certain you have
right now?

Which qualities are missing from your life in the present?

What would it take to bring these qualities into your life and
embrace them every day?

List three steps you will take to bring your life into alignment
with your values.

7
Building a
New Foundation

In preparation for your fresh, emerging life, you're going to need to lay the bricks of your new foundation. This is essential for your relationship with yourself, with others, and with your ex, as well as for your entire future. The necessary bricks for a solid base are a network of friends, having your finances in order, reserves of health, a strong purpose, and passionate interests.

Years ago when I was traveling in India, an earthquake struck in a heavily populated region nearby. Collapsing buildings buried thousands of people. Waiting in the airport for a flight connection, I spoke with some of the doctors and medical crews as they made their way there to help the rescue effort. I asked why and how this type of emergency occurs. The point made over and over was that the buildings that had fallen had been built with *poor foundations*.

This serves as a metaphor for situations that often arise in coaching sessions with my clients. Why do some people fall apart faster or harder than others when they are going through trying times? Because whether you are building a home, a relationship, or a new life, it is imperative to have firm underpinnings. If you don't, when your world shakes, *you* will come tumbling down.

Brick #1: Friends

One of the biggest challenges for singles is to not become isolated. It's important to reach out and make new connections while refreshing old ones. Friends can provide comfort and support in all kinds of ways, from helping you get a job to being there with a hug. You need a group of caring people who appreciate what you are going through, are there to help ground you, and to see who you are.

Flying home from overseas recently, I thought about what our national character looks like compared to other parts of the world. As Americans, we think of ourselves as independent people, and we're proud of our self-reliance. We often talk with admiration about those who "did it all by themselves."

But don't buy into that. Yes, we are independent, but if you believe that you have to do everything "all by yourself," you will be fighting an uphill battle and feeling guilty when you need support. All the great achievers in history had help on some level. It doesn't mean they didn't put hard work into accomplishing their dreams—but at many places along the way, they found the allies they needed to get where they wanted to go.

You need a support system. You need people who will help you network, introduce you to valuable connections, scout out opportunities for jobs, and explore housing options with you. You need places to go and people to go with. It is when you come together in a community of friends that you can accomplish the most.

My friend and fellow coach Christine Martin uses the example of geese in migration to stress the importance of a network. Instead of being isolated, consider the wisdom of geese:

As each bird flaps its wings, it creates an uplift for the bird immediately following. Create a flock of friends who share similar goals and values and can lift some of the burden you carry. They may not have dealt with or met some of the obstacles you are facing, but they can still lend encouragement, ideas, and introductions to other people. This flock helps you realize that you are not alone.

By flying in a V formation, the whole flock adds at least 71 percent more flying range than would be possible if each bird flew on its own. Recognize that by having a gathering of other people to "fly" with, you may have increased your range and possibility of achieving your goals and dreams by 71 percent. Having a group of friends can help you get to where you want to go faster, easier, and stronger.

When a goose falls out of formation, it suddenly feels the drag and resistance of trying to go it alone—and quickly gets back into formation to take advantage of the lifting power of the bird in front. Notice how it feels when you do not have friends around you. Does everything seem like more work? That's the wear and tear of trying to do it alone. Everything takes more energy.

When the head goose gets tired, it rotates back in the formation and another goose flies in the lead. Shift the load of some of the work it takes to accomplish your goals. Let others provide reinforcements. When you are part of a close group of friends and the constant responsibility and effort of being "out front" tires you, let your friends take over and be your networking directors for a while.

Geese honk from behind to encourage those up front to keep up their speed. Allow yourself to have a cheering section, honking from the back, when you are out there trying as hard as you can. You always do more and better with others calling out to you. And having someone to remind you that you are wonderful can be a tonic to the spirit.

When a goose becomes ill or is wounded and falls out of formation, two other geese fall out with that goose and follow it down to lend help and protection. They stay with the fallen goose until it is able to fly again or until it dies. Only then do they launch out on their own or with another formation to catch up with their group. Lastly, when you have been knocked down by illness or from others taking potshots at you, or your spirits are sagging for any other reason, you need at least two of your best buddies to hold your hand and bring you chicken soup. They do this because they are invested in your happiness and success. You would do the same for them because you are invested in their lives as well.

The qualities of the geese are compelling. They teach you how to support your friends and how to allow your friends to support you. This is key to your well-being when you are single again.

How do you put together a group of like-minded spirits? Besides close family, start reaching out to people who share similar spiritual beliefs. Extend yourself to the people you know and like at work. And find groups or organizations that participate in hobbies and recreational activities you love.

Everything is possible when you've got a flock of friends.

Brick #2: Finances

Divorces can be costly affairs. Whether your breakup involved lawyer fees and settlements or ended with minimal hassle, your financial situation today likely looks much different than it did when your partner was in the picture. Unraveling your finances from each other's and assessing your own financial footing are keys to a strong foundation.

Handling personal finances yourself is the way you become untangled from any knots in your relationship with your ex. If one of you is beholden to the other for money, it becomes a real challenge to have a sincere, ongoing interaction that isn't influenced by feelings of irritation, resentment, manipulation, or even anger. Financial independence is one of the most important bricks you need in order to put your friendship—and yourself—on a steady foundation. If you have difficulty managing what you have, seek professional help, educate yourself, and be discerning with your money.

Whatever your means of support, here is your new creed: live *below* your means. You may have material sacrifices to make and hard decisions to live with, so keep this rule written on your wallet. Living below your means gives you reserves. Often, financial advisors say you need six months of income in case you lose your job. I would say that you need at *least* a year's worth of personal income saved, especially after moving on from a breakup. When you have a strong financial safety net under you and you have made a practice of living frugally and simply, you are living your TAO. You are in the flow. When nature throws a boulder on your path, you have the financial means, as well as the calm, strength, and accumulated experience of perseverance, to move over or around it . . . and keep on flowing.

How you handle your finances has everything to do with your Take or beliefs about money. With beliefs leading to Action, and Action leading to Outcome, it helps to recognize the themes and phrases that have been lingering in our collective subconscious for centuries and that drive many of our choices in spending. Whatever the state of the world economy, you may hear some of the following comments, perhaps from your family of origin, the media, or your social environment:

- Money is the root of all evil.
- Women only want to marry rich men.
- You can't take it with you.
- I'll never get ahead.
- I'd rather be poor and happy than rich and miserable.

These beliefs can filter into your own consciousness, so it's worth asking yourself, What is my Take on money? Is it a positive one that brings you closer to your financial goals? These embedded thoughts or myths are hard to shake, so take a close look at your Take, and if it's one that doesn't serve you, reframe it into something affirmative. Doing so will lead you to the Action that will put you on a sturdier financial footing.

Here are some other triggers about money to look at:

Sales

Do you think you're saving money, even when you don't need what you're buying? Some people can go broke "saving" money at sales.

Do you go to "browse" and wind up buying something every time?

Do you take your new purchases home and never wear them or can't find a place to put them?

Does it sometimes feel like you have more "stuff" than you can remember you have . . . or than you can take care of?

Fashion and Fads

How many items do you buy because you see other people with them?

Do you feel entitled to everything you see and want?

Do you compare what you have to what celebrities have?

Broken

If something is broken, do you buy a replacement?

Do you recycle or learn to fix what's broken or just toss it out?

Stocking up

When you go to the grocery store, do you buy more fresh foods than you can eat? Do you find that you are constantly throwing away food that has gone bad?

Do you buy clothes that you want to wear when you have lost weight? Are those clothes still hanging in your closet with the tags on?

Do you find yourself buying the same things multiple times because you forgot you had them?

Think about your attitudes and habits and start discovering how you can alter your behavior if money is a consistent problem for you.

If you don't know where you need to take greater responsibility with your finances, answer these questions:

Do you rely on your ex for money?

Could you survive financially without your ex's support?

Do you spend money even when you don't have it?

Do you buy things you don't absolutely need, putting yourself in debt?

Do you have no money set aside for emergencies?

Do you charge your credit cards to the max?

Do you constantly have to borrow money from others?

Do you feel out of control with your spending?

Do you keep secrets from others about your spending habits?

Do you live above your means?

If you answered yes to any of the above, do not hide, run away, or deny that you need help. A problem with money has nothing to do with being a good person or a bad person. It means you have habits concerning your finances that are harming you. You may need to *downsize* your life—a lot—or readjust your expectations, find a new career, create work from home, or take a part-time job. It means you also need to reach out to get some counseling or expert financial advice.

On the other hand, you may have been the one in the marriage who handled the finances, and you may have done it well. But you probably also took a loss—of savings, retirement funds, or accrued investments—and you may be starting over in terms of building new reserves. Looking at ways to trim your expenditures and/or add extra income may require you to get creative, determined, and focused.

If you want to be truly independent, if you want to be completely in charge of your life, if you want to be calm but excited at the same time about your future, handle your finances. Even if you have to live with much, much less than you're used to, be smart with your money.

Brick #3: Health

You know the benefits of feeling well and taking good care of yourself, but it's often not a priority. A breakup can entail so much emotional exhaustion that your physical health becomes neglected. Sometimes identifying a new Take for your health requires nudges, reminders, and encouragement from friends.

Start with this checklist:

Have you had a physical checkup within the last year?

Do you get your teeth cleaned every six months?

Do you exercise for half an hour to an hour every day?

Do you get all your medical tests done for preventative care (mammogram, colonoscopy, blood work, chest X-ray, Pap smear, eye exam, bone density test, blood pressure, EKG, and others)?

Do you follow a balanced, healthy diet?

Do you regularly get eight hours of sleep at night?

Are you aware of your family's health history, and are you taking precautions where necessary?

One common issue regarding health matters and breakups is usually weight and how it relates to self-image. This is when you want to pay attention to your Take. What are some of the sneaky voices running through your mind that might be holding you back from your goals? What are you telling yourself and others?

My ex made fun of my weight all the time. That destroyed my self-esteem and just makes me eat more now!

I cooked for my ex to keep him happy, and even though he's gone, the eating has become a habit.

My weight issue is emotional, so I can't do anything about it.

I couldn't take time for myself when I was married, and now I'm so out of shape that I'll never get back to normal.

I don't have time to eat a healthy meal. I have coffee for breakfast and just grab a candy bar or fast food when I'm at work.

I've always been too busy with my career to exercise or eat well, and that caused my divorce.

Rewrite any negative scripts that are holding your spirit and body hostage. It's easy to run the thoughts of physical imperfection through your mind when you are inundated with media icons saying *thin is beautiful*. The Hollywood perception of what looks good and what doesn't, and comparing yourself to that standard, is unfair and unkind.

Good health is like having money in the bank for emergencies. In times of greater stress than normal, it's there to see you through the hard times. But if you are always burning the candle at both ends, when you hit a crisis, what do you think will happen if you don't have a reserve of energy and health? You have to take care of yourself all the time—not just when you are ill. Exercise, rest, healthy habits, checkups, and nurturing food are the preventative care you need.

Sylvia was a recently divorced, very attractive thirty-eight-year-old woman. Still beating herself up over her split from her husband, she was convinced she could have done more to save her marriage. Having been dedicated to her work, learning everything she could to climb the corporate ladder, she felt she'd neglected "self"-management.

Deep-seated feelings of inadequacy had triggered obsessive eating disorders, which she felt had contributed to her divorce. She worked all the time, fretted about her weight 24/7, was a fanatic about exercising, and had been anorexic and bulimic since high school. She had been seeing psychiatrists and therapists since she was fifteen years old.

"I have been struggling with my weight and self-esteem issues since I was a young child," she told me. "I used to be fat, and the other kids made fun of me. Then, in high school, I decided to lose weight, so I started to purge all my food after I ate it. I've been doing that all my life. The only thing that seems to help is if I run about ten miles a day. On the weekends, I do more.

"Maybe coaching could help me because I have so many things wrong with me. I want to get 'fixed' so I won't sabotage another relationship! My divorce was very painful, and it still haunts me that I didn't try harder to save my marriage."

I said, "Let's start off looking at what's right with you instead of what's wrong with you. Your entire focus is on the negative parts of your life."

I continued, "It's true that you're abusing your body to be thin. However, on the other side of that behavior is a *value* that has run off track. The value you're expressing is that you always try your best to do your best. That's a lovely value that is being misused and is working against you now.

"Perfectionism, which is part of trying your best, may have moved you on to more extreme measures. The behavior to achieve your goal of being 'perfect' and thin, however, has become a destructive habit. Let's see if we can redirect the energy you are expending in negative ways and put it toward doing something that's good for you. We'll set some goals to get you in shape in a positive, healthy way."

In the next weeks and months, Sylvia made agreements with me about what she would do for her health. We spent each session assessing all her strengths that she could use to help her achieve her goals, followed by assigning "homework." Identifying her inner voices that were critical, and shifting them to encouraging, affirming words made a huge difference. She also identified her values and got purposeful in her career. At the same time, she was under medical supervision for her eating disorder.

One day Sylvia said, "I am learning how to rest when I am tired, eat when I am hungry, and exercise when my body needs to move. It's starting to come in a natural way. When I hear the critical voice start to tell me that I am 'fat,' I shut it down and tell myself I am 'just right.' I am more focused on my work these days, and I'm loving the attention I'm getting from being good at what I do."

Sylvia made an enormous transformation. The energy that had been so self-destructive became her new positive life force. Now, no longer dieting, she exercises and eats healthy meals. She has been appointed director of a foreign office for her corporation, and she loves her new job and her new city. She no longer needs medication but continues to see her doctor every three months for checkups.

Sylvia called her ex and shared with him how she was doing. He told her he was pleased that they could have a conversation about this issue without fighting. Even though they have both moved on with their lives, they hope to stay connected as friends. Sylvia said it was satisfying to be able to talk with someone who had known her at her worst and share how she is now.

Sylvia's Take and Actions: I always try my hardest to do my best. I can reframe that quality into positive, constructive action. I now know how to achieve my goals without harming myself.

Brick #4: Purpose

Your foundation needs the brick of purpose to keep you steady on your feet. You can get through just about anything in life when you find meaning in what you're doing. Having purpose is, essentially, taking action to accomplish what's important to you. Purpose is why you get up in the morning.

Juliette went off to California after college to try to get into the entertainment business. She married a hospital technician, had a small flutter of activity in commercials, and then couldn't find any work. She tried for twelve years to find anything in acting. After many attempts to get into show business, she took a "temporary" job at an advertising agency, hoping her luck would change and she would succeed at an audition. She worked there for three years.

Juliette and her husband were never really passionate about each other, and as time went by, they grew more distant. She wasn't sure whether her marriage fell apart because of her unhappiness about her work or because she and her husband just weren't meant to be together. They parted amicably and found it easier to be friends than to be married.

About a year after they split up, Juliette could find no reason to stay in California. She did not like her current job, she had no acting auditions, and all her family was in the Midwest. She called them for help. Juliette's brother and sister drove to California to get her.

When thirty-four-year-old Juliette contacted me, she was full of shame about the way she thought her life had turned out. She told me, "I feel like a complete failure. I went off to California with people expecting—hoping—I would be successful out there."

"Tell me what it is you would have accomplished if you had succeeded in the film industry."

"I would have fulfilled a lifelong dream to be an actress and to be involved in acting productions. I wanted excitement, challenge, diversity, and admiration, and when I did come back, everyone would be happy to see me and be proud of me," she said.

"Are people happy to see you now?"

"Yes, but it isn't the same thing."

"I understand that you had a different goal in mind, but what is the essence of what you really, really want?" I asked.

Discovering what Juliette wanted, what her core values were, and finding her purpose were the central parts of our coaching sessions.

One day she said, "Actually, the more I think about it, the more I realize that I wanted the importance of working in films. But when I was near it and watched how it affected people's lives, I saw that the price to get there—if you ever did—was too high. I can see that what I want more is to have a rich life, with family and friends, and to find a way to have acting included in it. Now that I'm at home, I'm exploring how to bring those needs into my life."

She continued, "I think I might go back to school and get certified as a teacher and teach drama at the local college. They put on some great productions there. I could also act in local theater. I'd like to give back to the community some of what it gave me."

It did not take long for Juliette to get her life on track. She brightened as she talked, shifting her perception of who she once thought she wanted to be to what she wanted now. More important, Juliette had found her purpose that was in alignment with her other values.

Once Juliette set new goals and took action, she felt fulfilled. She no longer thought of her years in California as something she had failed at, but rather as a training ground to direct her to what she was currently meant to do. She continues to have friendly conversations with her ex. He is very happy for her growth.

Juliette's Take and Action: When I focus on my *values and purpose*, they help me realize what actions I want to take. For instance, I still love theater, but from a broader perspective. Instead of it being my whole life, it supports my new life—which is more whole than ever.

Having a purpose means having a goal while being in alignment and living from your values on the way to that goal.

Brick #5: Passionate Interests

There has to be some pizzazz in your life! One of the bricks you need under you is a source of passion. This is the energy that makes you sparkle all over.

Some interests are lifelong, and sometimes you may move on to others.

If you don't have any other interests besides your work and family, or you aren't energized by the ones you currently have, think about these questions:

What games did you love to play as a child? You may rediscover board games, cards, charades, checkers, or puppet shows. Or you may find that you are missing the fun of sports. Tennis, basketball, baseball, swimming, trampoline, soccer, snorkeling, or dancing may fill you with enthusiasm.

What were your favorite toys or props? They may sound silly when you think of them now, but remembering the toys that brought you joy as a child may hold clues to your passions today, as my client Fred discovered.

Fred told me he could find no enthusiasm for life, and I could tell that just by the sound of his voice on the phone. Divorced, he was no longer in touch with his ex. He had moved when he retired, had not made many new friends, and was looking for something to do.

After several sessions, I asked Fred, "What did you love to do as a child?"

"Oh, I don't know. The only thing I liked was watching cartoons."

"And what else?" I prodded.

"I don't remember," he droned. "I guess I liked to go out and ride my bike once in a while."

"And what else did you just love, couldn't stop doing, and were enthralled with?"

Out of the blue, a different voice emerged from Fred. It sounded alive as he said, "You know . . . I did have a little Brownie camera, and I loved to walk in the woods and take pictures of nature. I think that camera was my favorite thing in the world!"

"Fred," I said, "you need to go find that Brownie."

"I will, Tonja! I think I'll go to the camera store today and get a new camera and get back into it. Thanks!"

Fred found some new companions in his nature and photography work. He sent his ex a picture he had taken and wrote her a note. She wrote back a cordial response, and they have started to have a small level of communication.

Fred's photography brought him joy. What's your brick?

What activity have you always wanted to do but thought it sounded too crazy? I know a former professor who's in his sixties and tap dances on his deck outside every afternoon. This is the interest he started in his forties when he became single. It keeps him fit and it keeps him smiling.

As I mentioned in a previous chapter, my mother was terrified of horses but started riding in her fifties, which fueled her with energy for the rest of her life. She went on to become a rodeo queen and competed until she was eighty-five. Her passionate interest became her new identity.

I have friends and clients who have found all kinds of creative activities after their divorces or breakups. One person went to Peru to investigate the sightings of aircraft landings from outer space. One of my friends goes to the Caribbean and regularly swims with sharks. One client skydives and has become so good at it that she now is an instructor. Several friends have written books on subjects that I had no idea they knew so much about. Another client is a regular at a karaoke club and has singing parties at his house.

What lessons or classes have you always wanted to take? Here's your chance to reinvent your life and meet some new people. Consider foreign languages, mountain climbing, writing, acting, painting, bird-watching, music, dancing, fishing, parasailing, or anything else you have always wanted to do.

Get a local high school or college catalogue and investigate what the school offers. Or search online to find local clubs in your area. It's never too late to try anything.

What social or charitable organizations would you love to be a part of? Sometimes people can fulfill their need to heal others by belonging to charities that work for worthy causes. Look for the organization that represents your passion to help.

Volunteer at a hospital, homeless shelter, orphanage, animal rights group, or soup kitchen, or for a program for the physically challenged—whatever interests you.

A breakup gives you the chance to rebuild your life exactly the way you want it from the ground up. Identify the bricks that are missing in your personal foundation. Then get busy and take Action. That way you'll be standing on something rock-solid when building your new life.

Suggestions for Building Your Foundation

What are the bricks you need to work on? On a scale of one to ten, with one being the weakest and ten being the strongest, what number would you assign for the status of each of your individual bricks?

- Friends
- Finances
- Health
- Purpose
- Interests

Which brick is your weakest, and what can you do to strengthen it? In your journal, list three steps you can take to strengthen your brick. Then write the date by which you will take each step. Repeat this process for each brick until you are satisfied that each one is strong.

Part III

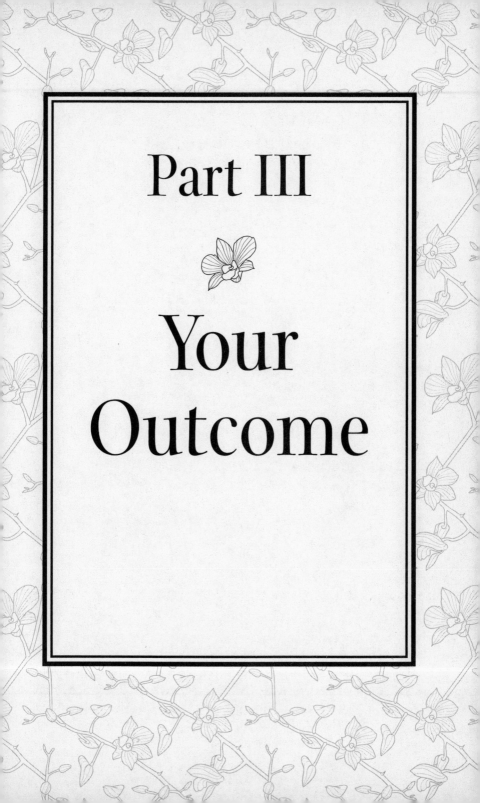

Your Outcome

8
Growing Your New Life

In your own personal TAO of Divorce, you are now at the point along the path where you experience the Outcome that has been determined by your Take and Actions. In a sense, your Take and Actions have planted the seeds that become your Outcome. It is at this stage that you get to reap the bounty of the life-affirming work you have done.

Have you ever visited a Japanese or Zen garden? In Chinese philosophy, the Tao, or "the Way," is based on principles of change and transition. These principles are no more apparent than in a Zen garden. As a matter of fact, Zen has its roots in Taoism, so I find a Zen garden to be especially useful in describing this particular point along your personal TAO, where you come into harmonious alignment with the changes you have experienced.

A Zen garden brings together elements such as water, stone, sand, empty space, plants, and trees into an ever-changing landscape. With slow-growing plants such as bonsai trees and moss, it is continuously sculpted and enhanced. It also serves up a host of delights with every season, making these living works of art well loved for their spiritual gifts.

Your life is not unlike a Zen garden. Lives, like gardens, are cultivated. The most serene, balanced, and thriving ones do not just happen. They require vision, patience, nurturing, and tending. The parallels to your life are endless. Both you and the garden need attention, commitment, and love. With a maturing inner wisdom gained from your divorce, you can now appreciate that there is nothing more fulfilling than spending your time and energy growing you.

Hopefully, your ex is busy cultivating his or her own garden. Depending on the level of your friendship, you may be assisting each other in important ways that produce the best in each of you. Only you can determine where and when mutual help is appropriate. Whatever your current relationship encompasses, the key is to stay connected to your own development. This is the optimum way to serve each other and everyone else in your world.

Gardening, like life, is a learn-as-you-go-and-grow project. Here are some steps to get you started.

Preparation

Preparation may be the most important part of a successful garden. Before you can plant, you have to consider the appropriate amount of sun, gather the necessary tools, enrich the soil, and have a plan.

How does this translate for your new life?

Sun

In a Zen garden are pockets of cool shade and stretches of glorious sunlight. Certain plants grow more easily and endure longer where it is warm and bright. When it comes to your life, are you standing in the light? Negative emotions could keep you a prisoner of darkness. This is why an enlightened perception of divorce serves you best. Freed from bitterness, anger, or guilt, divorce has become your catalyst to flourish in a healthy, light-filled atmosphere.

Tools

A Zen garden requires, among other tools, rakes, trowels, and pruning clippers for planting and maintenance. It's time to discover which tools you need to make your life easier and more rewarding. When you were taking stock in chapter 3, what did you discover in your personal assessment? It's important to be aware of what you currently have to work with and what you need to be equipped with to achieve your goals.

Are you looking for a new career? Do you need to take a course, get a particular degree, or find a mentor?

What about your social life? What steps can you take to meet new friends or even dates? Do you need a gym membership, dance lessons, a singles group, or a coach?

Are you sparkling from the inside in order to attract what you want? What can you do to find that passionate interest that makes you excited about life?

Thinking about the tools you need and getting them together are a big part of your future success.

Soil

Brilliantly colored Japanese maples, fragrant jasmine, towering bamboo . . . The majestic flora of a Zen garden all depend on the proper soil. How do you prepare the soil? Dig up the earth and add food, nutrients, and water. It's the heart of the garden.

What does this mean for you? *Dig in.* Don't skim, cut corners, or skip over anything that is important in your life. Your life is not different from a garden: you get back what you put into it. This is why you have to feed, enrich, protect, and tend to yourself—as much and as often as you need.

The wisdom you've gained from going through the breakup process should allow you to see when you need sustenance.

- Give your body what it needs: nutritious food, rest, and exercise.
- Educate your mind by reading, sharing, and listening to what others have learned on their path.
- Take care of your heart, using good emotional boundaries to protect it.
- Be on the lookout for pests who may nibble at your tender shoots and keep you from growing or stunt your growth.
- Nurture your soul with silence, prayer, and meditation.
- Plant yourself in a sunny place where you can embrace the light and have the best chance to grow.
- Become your own special part of nature, your own temple of solace, like a Zen garden.

This part of *preparation* contributes to your being a thriving, growing, beautiful human being.

Plan

A Zen garden needs soothing water, intriguing pathways, and places for quiet contemplation. It all starts with the gardener's vision, which then becomes a plan. With dedication and focus, the plan is transformed into reality. How do you envision your garden? What do you want to achieve? Do you have the energy and resources to sustain and maintain what you have planned? Obviously, a successful garden takes thought.

Have you given yourself this kind of consideration? Do you have a vision for your new life? What is your plan to bring your vision into reality? Perhaps it is time to alter, expand, buff up, or develop a whole new picture, and then plan how you will get it. The following questions will help you focus and get started:

What would you like to change in your life?

What would make your life better?

Envision the *perfect* life for you. How is it different from your life now?

What do you need to do to bring the two pictures into alignment?

Just as you would design a plan for a garden, what does the plan for your new life look like?

Whom can you talk with about your plan to help you gain clarity?

What one step can you take today that would bring you closer to your vision?

Developing a plan and fulfilling it requires some practical actions. This is the way you bring yourself an inspired life.

Plant

Gardeners relish the time for planting. This is a satisfying step; they know that soon they will start to witness growth.

How can you plant the seeds for the life that you want? Begin with sowing the seeds in your own mind and heart first. Then move on to planting your ideas and goals in the minds of others.

- Network with friends, family, colleagues, teachers, mentors, and everyone you interact with, telling them what you want. Whether it is a new home, job, social life, gym, or even a pet, don't be shy and don't give up. Be determined.
- Ask people for names of contacts. Go places where you can meet them. Whether you are looking for a job, a volunteer position, a particular item, or simply more information about one of your passions, networking brings results. Résumés, applications, questionnaires, letters of inquiry, or recommendations often go nowhere unless they have someone's name on them. Always follow up with a call.
- Show up at conferences, seminars, retreats, conventions, courses, and anywhere else that's appropriate to get more information and more people to talk to. This is how you build your practical, as well as spiritual, network.
- Regularly check print and internet media for what you are looking for—information, items, people, connections—and respond appropriately. Be diligent.
- Fill out questionnaires, information sheets, or applications for what you want with care, style, quality, and authenticity.
- Keep becoming an expert at what you are interested in.
- Focus on and visualize your desire every day. Imagine seeing it as magnetically drawn to you, feeling the pull of energy.

With your preparation complete and your seeds of possibility planted, you are ready to move into the next stage. Your garden is about to grow.

Patience, Growth, and Rewards

After the Zen gardener has planted the ferns and trees, started the moss, and sown the seeds, the plants need time to grow. First they sleep before they start to creep and eventually leap. The dedicated and respectful gardener shows up every day to do what is necessary to nurture each stage.

What does this mean for you? Practice patience. Gardens cannot be rushed.

Patience

Some people want to see results right away. But, of course, gardens don't work that way. The growth process requires patience and continuing care.

You may begin to feel that you have done all your preparation work and told people what you want but nothing is happening. You have to trust that something *is* happening, even if you can't see it yet. Your ideas are germinating inside you, as well as with the rest of your network. Trust that the process will unfold in its natural way.

Focus. Keep doing what needs to be done. Don't be lured into other projects or distractions right now. It may be tempting to go start something else or accept less than you want, but give what you started a chance to grow.

Feed. Continue to feed information and requests to others, attend events that relate to you or your cause, keep honing your skills, interact with new and old contacts, and nurture your network. Feed your body and spirit what they need.

Weed. This has to be done on a continual basis, no matter what cycle you are in. Weed out noisy, needy, demanding people who distract or drain you. Everyone knows that weeds choke out healthy growth, block the light, and feed off your hard work. Eliminate them to allow your garden to thrive.

Conserve. Protect your energy by using it for what you want and need to do. There is not an unlimited supply of it, so set your priorities and keep to them.

Believe. Believe you will get what you want, believe that you deserve it, and know that all the work you have invested will come back to you.

Pause. Most of us don't pause long enough to appreciate the work we are putting in. Take time to enjoy the sunshine while you tend to what you have planted.

Growth

The first signs of your hard work appear during this stage. But, ironically, this is where some people lose their direction and balance—especially if they have never planned and planted a full garden before. Seeing the creepers *is* wonderful, but they are only the beginning.

The hard part for you may be to continue working for your goals and not stop at the first few green shoots and think that this is it. For example, the first job offer or the first date or the first new house you look at will probably just be the start of what you have planted to grow.

Remember to

- Keep working. Growth has to be constantly managed. Something new sprouts up every day, and you need to check it out to see what it needs.

- Continue to feed, weed, and tend to what you have started. Do not wander far off or for very long. This is the time to be steadfast.
- Pay attention to the new skills, confidence, and maturity you are gaining as you go through this process.

Rewards

If your garden is flourishing, it means you have stayed loyal and dedicated to what you planned and worked for. You have learned to be proficient with your tools, you know how to tend and nurture what you started, and you are enjoying the rewards of what you have grown. Bravo!

Just as a beautiful garden needs continuing attention, your life needs the same. You still have to weed, prune, water, and feed what you have sown. You have great choices now, so you can study your results with a careful and selective eye. Take a moment every day to recognize and appreciate what you have accomplished.

Did you get what you planned for?

What do you need more of and less of?

What was the most important thing you learned?

This garden analogy is a strong reminder of how life works in stages. Most clients in coaching can relate to this idea from their own experience. But sometimes it takes actually living through the steps and getting to that important goal for it to become real.

My client Allison was like many other people who are divorced, have been single for a while, and feel somewhat isolated. She wanted to meet people and maybe start dating.

She was athletic, petite, and youthful looking. She had gotten married when she was eighteen, divorced twenty years later, and had two teenage boys. She had worked hard during those years, putting her husband through school and raising her sons. But over time, she and her husband grew apart. After a year of marital counseling, Allison asked him for a divorce. She said she felt trapped in an unfulfilling life.

She wanted to go to school, travel, and discover more of the world. She wanted out of the negativity of her marriage. In short, she was preparing for a new *garden*. She was ready to step out of the shadows and into the *sun*. She was scared but brave. Longing to meet new people and find friends, she said she had never socialized with anyone except those she knew with her ex. After her divorce, she moved across town, started a new job, and was going to night school. She was beginning to give herself some of the things she had always wanted.

"How do I meet new people?" she asked. "It seems that everyone around me is involved with their own friends, and I don't know where to begin. I feel somewhat overwhelmed."

I said, "With a new home for yourself and a new job, it sounds like you have chosen a sunny spot to begin realizing some of your dreams. You are also beginning to have a *vision*, like wanting to have a social life. The most important part of this vision, however, is to feel good about what you are doing—every day—and the nurturing relationship you have with yourself. It's hard to find good friends if you are not a friend to yourself first."

Allison asked, "How exactly do I do that?"

"Well, besides all the goals we have talked about and have been developing for your health, career, finances, and family, try some indulgences. You've always been a very responsible, get-the-job-done kind of a person. Why not try sleeping in on Sunday morning if you feel like it? Instead of your usual trip to the gym, take a walk by the lake, buy yourself a coffee, and sit on a bench, people-watching. Feed the ducks; go to the horse races; have a chocolate brownie." She needed to spend some time enriching the soil of her soul.

Allison shared that indulging her whims felt very foreign to her. "Up until now, I didn't have time to do those things," she said. "If I dared to let myself think about them, I felt guilty. Everything I did was for everyone else. Maybe that's why I never learned social skills. The people who came to our house were mostly just family."

"Discovering your social life takes some simple *tools*," I told her, "and here is the most important one: being friendly. Start with the people where you work and those who are in your classes. Following that, in order to have friends, you have to get out of the house and go places."

In subsequent sessions, we talked about what qualities she had to offer, as well as what she was looking for in a good friend.

"This time around, you get to choose the people you want to be with. The tool of learning to be discriminating about whom you invite into your life is important now. Make a list of the character traits you admire and strive to have. Other people with similar standards to yours will be the most appealing to you. This is also a good time to use everything you learned from your marriage and divorce to make yourself more aware of what works for you and what doesn't."

"That's great," she said. "How do I get started?"

"Single women who want to start socializing after a breakup or divorce expect people—and especially men—to come and find them. That doesn't work anymore. When you're old enough to be out of school, you have to find a different pool to select from. That is the concept that seems to keep singles frozen. They don't know where to go.

"A great tool for meeting people is to find an activity you are excited about. The big shift that has to occur is this: you have to take responsibility for the quality of your social life. You can't wait for other people to come knocking on your door. You have to create the opportunities where they can meet you."

"People know I'm alone, but not that many of them ask me to do things," Allison said.

"You have to stretch yourself. You're waiting for life to come to you.

"Develop a *plan*. Look in your local newspaper for something you'd like to attend. Write on a calendar the names of people you'll call to ask to join you. Plan at least four outings a month."

She had to plant the seeds in order to grow what she wanted. And then, just as seeds require *patience* as they germinate, she had to give her requests time to develop from possibilities into realities. Eventually, those sleeping seeds start to *grow*.

"If you're dating," I told her, "don't fall into a relationship with the first person you meet. Dating is the first sign that your networking is starting to produce results.

"Settling too soon for the first people who show up in your life to be friends or dates is a pattern I see frequently. The 'scarcity' belief causes people to compromise their dreams before they've had a chance to learn how to be discriminating. You want to select friends who are a positive influence in your life."

Allison refreshed her social skills, knocked herself out meeting new people, turned down the volume of her inner negative voice, and tuned in to all the ways she could accomplish her goals. These were some of the ways she learned to be a better friend to herself.

Allison became so absorbed in her growth and her exciting life that she found it easy to be civil with her ex and his new wife. He is still a bit chilly with her, but the common interest of their sons motivates Allison to remember her boundaries and be patient with his temperament.

Allison kept meeting people. The day arrived when her social "garden" began to *leap*. More and more friends came her way, with the quality and choices of her dates growing, until, of course, she had a full calendar.

This was how Allison learned to cultivate her own garden.

Bonuses from the Garden

The way you care for your garden today brings you rewards tomorrow. But while you're tending your garden, there are many other benefits you experience:

Energy. Taking action always brings you more energy. It breaks up any deadlock in areas that may feel stagnant. You are also doing something that brings you a tangible result. More energy equals more sparkle; more sparkle means you attract more of what you want.

Less stress. When you are actually *doing* something to enhance your life, you are less anxious. You're not waiting for someone to do it for you, waiting to get "lucky," or waiting for opportunity to come knocking. You are taking responsibility for your life and your happiness, which relieves stress.

Contribution. You have no idea how much you are inspiring the people around you. You may not be aware that you are being watched, but your determination and get-up-and-go attitude are infectious. Your example alone gives others energy, hope, and ideas to work on their own life. This in itself is reason enough to be doing what you are doing.

Attention. You are learning to pay attention to the important details in your life: attention to how to get what you want and attention to your own needs. You now know that you cannot abandon yourself and expect anything to grow or turn out well.

Patience. Just as the garden takes time and patience, you need the same. It is easy to give up, feel that nothing is working, and halt your efforts. If you have planted a fruit tree, it may take years to produce. Give yourself this same consideration in your goals. The various opportunities you are seeking have different time requirements.

Realism. Sometimes your goals require a certain benign "ruthlessness." You have to prune the smaller or weaker growth to let the more promising sprouts emerge and have a chance. You are required to find the wisdom to know what should go and what should grow, and in doing that, you are being realistic.

Control. Even though you have a great deal of control over how your life and garden turn out, there are times when you have none. Bad weather, catastrophes, and events beyond your imagination can happen. Gardens and lives are susceptible to pests and droughts and surprise freezes. Unexpected things happen, and from this you learn to adapt and be flexible. You have to expand in maturity in order to gracefully roll with things that are out of your control.

Keeping agreements. When you plant a garden and want it to succeed, you have a built-in set of agreements with it. It's a perfect reminder of what happens when you don't take care of yourself. Beautiful greenery can be choked out by weeds, wilt from insufficient water, or starve for lack of nutrition. A healthy, flourishing garden can't thrive without constant attention. It needs to be cultivated, nurtured, tended, and appreciated—just like you do. That means you have to keep agreements with yourself and for yourself. You have to show up—over and over.

Forgiveness. No matter how hard you try, you will make mistakes; this is a given. But when you forgive yourself, knowing you gave it your best effort, you are also more forgiving of the human errors of others. This is how you grow yourself to be bigger, better, and stronger.

The Zen garden is an apt metaphor when you are starting a new life and beginning to live life from your new TAO. This primeval example has everything you need to know as you set out to reinvent yourself. Now is the time to plant your seeds of possibility. It's time to plan your work and get busy, because your future depends on what you do now.

What is your new TAO?

- Your Take: My life is like a gorgeous garden—a work of art in constant motion, change, and growth.
- Your Actions: I take all the necessary steps to keep my commitments to myself and to keep growing.
- Your Outcome: Each day is a revelation as I flow, unfold, and keep emerging into another surprising, exhilarating stage.

In the meantime, the kindness and patience you learn from tending your garden will be reflected in everything you do.

Suggestions for Growing Your Life

When you set out to accomplish your goals, keep a journal to include thoughts on some of the following questions:

What are you doing to prepare yourself?

How will you remove any lingering darkness and bring yourself more light?

Which of your tools will help you get what you want?

If you need more tools, what will you do to get them?

How will you dig in and feed, nurture, and tend to yourself?

What will you plant?

What is your plan?

What are your actions, thoughts, and emotions during the time your garden germinates, shows signs of growth, and finally leaps?

What other bonuses are you getting from the gardening process?

What positive skills, knowledge, or insights did you learn from your relationship with your ex that can be transplanted to your new garden?

9
Getting What You Want

As you fully embrace the Outcomes that are the result of your new TAO, you will find yourself on the brink of a thrilling time. You can now see that you have the power to create the life you want and deserve. *Focused energy* is the key to your fulfillment.

Using the power of energy and focus—and not relying on anyone else to provide for your needs—you become capable of delivering your own dreams for the future. This self-empowerment will erase any lingering strands of hurt, anger, or disillusionment from your divorce.

Getting what you want by using the power of concentration and energy takes the following steps, which I've discovered through personal experience:

1. *Decide:* Choose a goal.

2. *Focus:* Put all your attention on what you want.

3. *Visualize:* Picture it over and over.

4. *Imagine:* Feel what it would be like to have what you want.

5. *Act:* Take the actions necessary to get it.

6. *Believe:* Know you will get it.

7. *Surrender:* Let the universe deliver what you want. If it doesn't appear, it's only because something better is coming.

I came upon this knowledge quite by accident. After my divorce, I was looking for an interest that was exciting. Having put my responsibilities in order, I was ready for something that captured my imagination. One night a newspaper article about how to win contests caught my eye. I felt a strange ripple of electrical current go through me, as if someone had switched on a light.

The piece was a short interview with a local woman who talked about how she focuses her attention on winning contests. The central theme was to suspend doubt and be willing to open up to a new way of thinking. I was ready for this. It was time to discover how to give myself what I wanted.

After spending time learning how to really concentrate and studying how positive energy could influence an outcome, I wrote down those seven steps to getting what I want.

Within days of making this list, I saw the contest I wanted to win: a week in Holland, all expenses paid for two. I had to write in fifty words or less why I should represent my country at the celebration of two hundred years of trade between the Netherlands and the United States. I thought, *Yes! Why shouldn't I?*

The idea of a trip to Europe was something I could definitely get enthused about. Whether I won it or not didn't seem to matter; I hadn't felt this kind of excitement in a long time.

After ten drafts, I sent the essay in—slathered with intention and light. My energy level was so high that I couldn't seem to keep quiet. I went on endlessly to people about what I was doing.

So many of them gave me frozen smiles that I finally stopped talking about it. I could almost read their thoughts: *So it's come to this. Her divorce has caused her to lose her mind.*

One of my friends is a therapist, and I was certain she would understand. I told her about the contest. She nodded and smiled and looked utterly confused. Obviously, she didn't get it either.

Six weeks later, the special-delivery letter came that said I had won. I couldn't believe it, and—at the same time—I *had known* it would happen. I called my therapist friend to invite her to Europe with me. She was in shock.

It was the first time out of the country for either of us. All the way over on the plane, I kept talking about positive energy and how to use it. She listened. She was patient. But she just couldn't fathom what I was saying.

In Holland, we saw the art of the Dutch Masters, we traveled to villages where they gave us gifts and toasts and banquets, and we even met the queen of the Netherlands.

The last night in Amsterdam, a large group of American and Dutch guests assembled at an exposition hall for more entertainment. When we entered we were each given a Dutch hat and a ticket for a raffle—the prize was a diamond stickpin from the queen. I thought, *Great! Another opportunity to test my concentration and focus.*

Finally, it was time to draw the ticket. Unfortunately, my friend had stepped out for a minute, so she missed the show that was about to happen. I looked up and down the long dining table and said, "Hey, guys, I really want to win this. All of you are sitting here sparkling in your gems tonight, and I don't have a diamond stickpin to my name. Could you picture my number with me?"

I think they agreed because they were nice people, they thought the idea was funny, and they probably didn't think it would work. There was one lady at the table, however, who spoke up and said, "Noooo. *I* want to win it." (Unfortunately for her, she was too late. I had asked first.)

So there we were, fifteen men and women wearing our little Dutch hats, holding hands and closing our eyes. When they called my number it was like a high-voltage current hit us at the same time. We jumped in the air and yelled.

Half-startled, half-crazy with excitement, I jumped all the way to the podium to collect my jewel, my Dutch hat wings flapping like Peter Rabbit's ears. My crew of concentrators was in the background, jumping and flopping too.

When my friend returned and I told her what had happened, the color in her face went past the point of ashen, and she said, feebly, "You're scaring me."

She finally got it.

It *is* overwhelming when you discover the power to create what you want. And when you do, you'll probably be flooded with feelings all the way from fear to unimaginable triumph.

Becoming a Believer

Effectively teaching or communicating how to focus energy is essential in coaching. Some people are a tough sell, though, like the chemistry professor I worked with who argued that the whole concept was unscientific and therefore couldn't possibly succeed. Because he had nothing to lose, he decided to try it anyway. He told me the only reason he finally agreed to do it was because "I'm so miserable and lonely, I'll try anything."

Don worked at a prestigious university. His wife had left him for a younger man, and he wasn't dealing well with the hurt, embarrassment, and sense of betrayal. He was a brilliant, sweet guy trapped inside a negative mind-set. He wanted to meet someone, but his Take on dating was that it was impossible for him to start over. He said what so many people say after a divorce: "I can't learn to date at my age. No one would want me, and besides, all the good women are taken."

Cracking his cemented beliefs took months. We worked on his TAO of Divorce. He listened for his negative voice and began to consciously rescript his Take.

Don became diligent at using boundaries in order to relate to people better. Not understanding how he crossed the personal lines of others, and unaware of the impact of his words and actions, he had found himself in the middle of a lot of upsets in the past. Now, armed with new knowledge, he was starting to build stronger friendships while reaching out to people.

We focused on his strengths and deepened his awareness of his values. Slowly and gently, Don was beginning to shift his opinion of himself and consider the new opportunities that were opening up for him.

Introducing some new Actions, I suggested that he look for pictures of what he wanted and put them on a bulletin board where he'd see them before he fell asleep and when he woke up. He did this but hid them under the bed when his daughters visited. He had trouble not making fun of this idea even though after just a few weeks, he began to experience some of the images he had posted.

After he went rowing on a lake with a date he had met on the internet, I asked if he had that picture on his board. He said yes but dismissed it as a coincidence and as something he might have done anyway, even though he hadn't had a date since before he was married.

He started dance classes at a local studio. When he went home, he realized that he had cut out a picture of two people dancing together—dancing was something he had always wanted to do. He was having more fun than ever before.

Dating, dancing, rowing, and other activities began to make Don a happy guy. It led him to finally be able to talk to his ex about their children and other matters pertinent to their lives. His hurt and anger were dissipating.

Other pictures that were on his board also became realities. Finally, he told me he was ready to meet someone fabulous, fall madly in love, and live in Europe for most of the year. He wanted an apartment in the States that he could come back to frequently so he could visit his children. "This seems like a big fairy tale to me, so I've been afraid to say it. But since these other things have been happening, maybe this can happen too."

We spent time looking at what kind of person he wanted to share his life with and listed some of his requirements. We also began to picture him finding a job in Europe. Don began to develop a vision for his future. I suggested that he now find pictures that would represent not only the life he wanted but how he would *feel* with that life. Still a little skeptical, he did it.

What was Don's Outcome? Within a year, he got exactly what he visualized. I am happy to report that he met someone from Belgium, they fell deeply in love, and they are creating their schedules to live in Europe most of the time and return often to their apartment in San Francisco.

Don no longer feels bad when he thinks or talks about his ex. He considers it his good fortune that she moved on and he was forced to find a new life, because Don absolutely loves his new life!

What is Don's new TAO?

- Don's Take: Negative thoughts and words only bring me more negativity. I have the power to shift my Take into something good that will serve me better. I am grateful I was pushed into finding my new life.

- Don's Actions: When I want something, I need to focus my energy, form a positive Take, and take the steps to make it happen.
- Don's Outcome: When I have a positive Take and assume responsibility for what I want through my Actions, my Outcome is always perfect—whatever it turns out to be.

The Irresistible Appeal of People Who Get What They Want

WARNING: When you begin to use focus, shifting your mind to what is now possible, you will become extremely attractive to everyone and everything. More and more people will want you to be on their committee, team, or board. Others will ask you to be their friend, their date, or their mate. Opportunities are going to come flying at you as you become a magnet. Your challenge is to stay grounded, clear, and *selective.*

Your ex will start looking at you differently, possibly also becoming more attracted to you. Remember your boundaries and reread chapter 4. Unless you want to rekindle your romantic relationship with your ex, you are going to need some strong lines between you.

I often tell divorced clients, "The more you practice these steps, the more positive responses you are going to receive . . . including from the opposite sex."

But my client Harry found that hard to believe. I told him, "Honest, Harry—women are going to be following you around town and lining up outside your door."

"Oh *sure*, Tonja! I can just see that now," he scoffed. "It's never happened before, and I know for a fact that it never will!" This was Harry's old Take.

Harry had been married twice. He was cordial with his first wife and not on speaking terms with his second. His problem was that he didn't think he was attractive to women; therefore, he settled for the first one who would go out with him. I told him we would do things differently this time. Settling for someone is a guarantee of relationship failure.

Harry needed a better relationship with himself before he could find one with a woman. We affirmed his strengths, took the focus off what he perceived to be his weaknesses, and found new activities to think about. Harry's new Actions were these: He joined a tennis team, started going to the gym, and got a dog, which he walked every morning and night. Harry learned about body language, eye contact, and being friendly with strangers. When he saw neighbors on his walk, he began to say hello and even stop for a chat. He also joined his tennis friends for a drink after their games. Harry loved this growing camaraderie and was enjoying himself socially for the first time in his life.

He added some new pieces to his wardrobe and was finding it increasingly easy to strike up a conversation with anyone—including women. In fact, he got so good at acknowledging people that he began to be the most popular guy in his small town.

Six months later, Harry called and said, "I thought you were crazy when you said women would be chasing after me. I really did. I wasn't trying to be rude; I just thought you were nuts! But, honest, women are following me *everywhere!*"

"Of course they are, Harry. I knew they would once we shifted your negative Take and got you feeling terrific. No one can resist that magnetic energy you have now."

Harry finds it even easier to relate to his first wife, and he doesn't have time for angry words or feelings toward his second. That's because he can't get over the fact that everyone's just wild about Harry! Harry is more than a little pleased with his Outcome.

All It Takes Is Being Open to the Idea

When I was divorced, my children watched how I focused on what I wanted. Because they were young and hadn't yet absorbed the negative tapes that say you can't do something, they just assumed they could create whatever they wanted to. So they did.

Their response was, "Awesome, Mom! This is fun!"

My son loved food, and he craved big quantities of it. This was his focus as a child, even though he was wiry. In different raffles, he won a giant hoagie the length of the living room, a huge cookie the size of a coffee table, and other meals and snacks along the way, as well as tickets to sports or music events. My daughter won prizes with her dog and wrote essays about her family that gave her money and publicity. All of this proved to me that you could pass the concepts of focus and energy on to others if they are open to them.

I taught a seminar for divorced women on empowerment a few years ago. For almost all the women, the divorce wounds were fresh and they had few kind things to say about their exes. In their minds, most of the problems in their past relationships belonged to the ex.

I explained positive thought, focus, and how energy works: "When you learn how to attract what you want, you won't feel needy, dependent, or even bitter about your breakup."

The discussion that followed was full of doubt . . . with a trickle of hope.

"Why don't we go around the room and each person can tell us what she wants? We can all give each other energy," I said.

The first woman to speak up said, "Well, I've always wanted to go to Hawaii, but since I'm broke, have a hard time paying my bills, and don't have a husband now to help me, that's not going to happen anytime soon." We all pictured Lorraine in Hawaii.

One woman said she would like to get back into her art. Since her divorce, she had been overwhelmed with taking care of her family and had given up doing what she loved.

Another woman in her thirties said she wanted to believe that someday she would find her soul mate, get married, and have a family.

When she said that, someone else, who was in her fifties, said she would love to meet a wonderful man, have a great relationship, and travel.

Someone else spoke up and said she was sick of her job, didn't make enough money, and worked all the time. She wanted to earn more money and be happier in her career.

We sent energy to each person when she made her desires known. But some women didn't say anything, since they didn't believe in what we were talking about.

A week later we met again. Lorraine was the first to share.

"You're not going to believe this, but the wildest thing happened this week! My college roommate, whom I hadn't heard from in ages, called me to ask if I wanted to go to Hawaii with her—all expenses paid. She and her husband had planned this trip, and now he can't go. There was a plane ticket, a hotel room, and all meals would be paid for. I couldn't believe it!"

We all cheered and clapped and asked when she was going. She said, "Oh, I can't possibly go. There's no way I can work it out."

"Why not?" we all asked. Lorraine didn't really have an answer—just feeble excuses. I could see that I had more work to do with Lorraine.

This is what happens when we haven't grown ourselves big enough to allow wonderful things to happen for us. When we are stuck in limited thought, don't believe we deserve a terrific life, and stay attached to the idea of struggle, we get overwhelmed when our dreams start to come true. After all, who would we be without our story of pain and hardship? Who would feel sorry for us and give us comfort? How would we be different from everyone else?

Believing we have suffered more than others gives us an excuse to not try. It's also a perfect reason to indulge our addictions. These are some of the reasons why people stay imprisoned in uninspired lives.

The woman who wanted to get back into her artwork went home that night and got started. At the next meeting she brought her latest painting to show the group. It was magnificent. Today she is not only still producing but even selling some of her work.

Two years after that seminar, the woman in her thirties is married and has a baby, the woman in her fifties has met the love of her life and they spend their time traveling together for both work and pleasure, and the woman who hated her job now works for herself and makes five times the salary she used to make.

Four of these five people also now have better relationships with their exes. Once they discovered how to give themselves what they wanted, their grudges, resentments, and bitterness dissolved.

As far as I know, the people who did not speak up are still doing what they have always done: living their self-limiting beliefs.

Five years after my Dutch trip, I met my husband, Vik. Naturally, I had focused my energy on the qualities I was looking for in a romantic/life partner—qualities I had appreciated in others but had never seen all in one man! I was clear that I wouldn't settle.

When Vik and I found each other, I was still teaching seminars on creativity. When he accompanied me to them, whether the audience was large or small, someone would always raise his or her hand and ask, "How did you meet your husband?" This would bring nods and cheers from the group; I suppose they could see how connected we were. Clearly, everyone wants to know how to create their dreams—and *attract* their dreams.

Shortly after I met Vik, I told him what I had learned about energy. He didn't really get it.

I decided I'd have to demonstrate the process to him when I got the opportunity. A couple of weeks later, we were at an event where they were raffling off a cowboy hat.

"Vik," I said, "you're in a family of cowboys now. You need a hat. I'm going to win it for you."

"OK ... sure ... that'll be nice," he said. He clearly didn't understand. So I

Step #1: *Decided* I wanted the cowboy hat.
Step #2: *Focused* on winning it.
Step #3: *Visualized* Vik wearing it.
Step #4: *Imagined* excitement when they called my number.
Step #5: *Acted* by buying a raffle ticket.
Step #6: *Believed* it was going to happen.
Step #7: *Surrendered* by savoring the moment.

When I won his hat, at first he and his friends were shocked. But soon they began to claim it was a coincidence, told me there weren't that many people trying for it so the odds were pretty good for me, and gave me a lot of other "logical" explanations. I sighed and gave it a rest.

Several weeks later, we were at a banquet in a hotel. They were raffling off a weekend getaway for two. *That sounds terrific,* I thought. *We needed a short vacation.* I told my husband I was going to win it.

"Good," he said, "Good. Yes, I think you should do that. That would be lovely."

I thought, *He still doesn't believe me; as much as he'd like to, he doesn't understand.* I asked him to concentrate on my ticket number anyway. The ballroom was packed with people who became totally quiet when the organizers called out the numbers. Vik was startled when we won it. In fact, he looked a little rattled because, in a room filled with five hundred people, he could find no logic or favorable odds or coincidences.

We had such a good time on our holiday weekend that I told him, "I think we need a longer vacation. Let's go away for a week to an island. I'm going to look for an opportunity for a tropical trip."

"Great idea!" he enthused. He was finally getting there. A few days later, I found a contest for a week in Aruba for two. This was a national contest, so I knew it would take strong focus to win it. We both sent the entry forms our energy. And he didn't feel the least bit silly doing it.

On the way to Aruba, a flight attendant asked the passengers a trivia question. I'm usually terrible at Trivial Pursuit, but for some reason, I was the only one who knew the answer. I won a bottle of champagne. When we got to our hotel, we had a lot of great things to toast, including focused energy.

If you want to begin using your focus for what you want, it's best to start off with something simple, where the odds are pretty good for you. Keep trying until you have success. This will build your confidence and belief that it can happen.

Start by visualizing the perfect pair of shoes you need and finding them on sale; a parking spot in front of the store you want to go to; or the amount of money you need in your account to pay an extra bill this month. It helps if you do the visualizing, picturing, and intending *before* you get to the shop or the parking lot or the bill's due date. When you accomplish your first successes, don't stop there. Set new goals and move on to the next ones.

When You Don't Get What You *Think* You Want

Sometimes you may not get what you think you want. Staring disappointment in the face, it may be hard to believe that *not* getting what you think you want is a blessing in disguise. But that is often the case.

When I was an educational consultant, there was a time when I was working hard toward creating, funding, and airing a parenting TV spot. The concept of the "edu-tainment" minute was to demonstrate how to have fun with children while teaching educational concepts. I was prepared for this project, having written books for parents, teachers, and children and having made award-winning recordings and videos in this field.

I put huge amounts of energy into this goal, and lots of wonderful people stepped forward and invested their time and talents as well. I gave it my laser-beam focus. In the end, we were able to raise about half the money and sponsors needed, but not the rest. What I thought was a brilliant plan fell flat, and for a period of time, so did I.

I thought perhaps I had lost my ability to manifest what I wanted. It was discouraging and confusing, and I felt bad for the people I had involved. It took considerable effort to not be influenced by some of the negative thoughts that permeated my mind, like "You need more talent," or "Someone else could do it better." I had to fight these mean little voices like crazy to keep them from taking away my optimism about life and my confidence.

This disappointment was partly responsible for me deciding to go back to school, becoming a coach and columnist, and reinventing my life. I have never been happier or more fulfilled. What I learned from that intense experience was to take time to find out where I might be out of alignment. Without realizing it then, I was tired of what I was doing and was unconsciously searching for something different. I didn't really *want* the TV spot, because it would have kept me stuck.

Ultimately, when things don't come your way, you have to know there is a greater energy and intention at work. The path is not always well lit, but something better is coming to you; just because you can't see it right away doesn't mean you should give up on the process.

The aspect of focusing on what you want is important to your growth. It helps you get clear about what you're doing and why. It helps you look deeply within and discover whether you are in sync with yourself. And it teaches you that when you work in harmony with your talents, experiences, and inner wisdom, you will be in command of shaping your own destiny.

Once you master the process of positive thoughts and focus, you can apply it across the board to anything you choose. Best of all, when you tap into this strength, you are relieved of all thoughts of clinging to anyone else to provide you with what you want.

As you move forward in your new empowered life, take a look at your former TAO and your different, emerging one. Can you see and feel the difference? Getting what you want becomes part of your new flow. It starts to become effortless, calm, and just the way it should be: divine.

Suggestions for Getting What You Want

1. **Set your goal.**
   - Write a list of some of the things you've been wanting. (They don't all have to be material things.)
   - Choose one and focus on it.
   - Start with something simple so that when you get it, it will raise your confidence.

2. **What will it look like when you have what you want?**
   - Imagine getting what you want.
   - Describe what it looks like in your notebook.
   - Cut out a picture of what you want and look at it in the morning and at night before you fall asleep.
   - Don't worry yet about how you're going to succeed. Just keep your eyes and ears open for the opportunity coming your way.

3. **Take action.**
   - Investigate what steps you need to take to accomplish your goal.
   - Write them down in your notebook and provide details.

4. **Believe you can have it.**
   - Keep looking at the picture, sensing you have what you want.
   - Think about it as if it's real.
   - Share your thoughts with a good friend.
   - Keep pictures in your mind of what you want, and know that you'll get it.

5. **Surrender.**
   - Let it go.
   - Keep visualizing, believing, and sending out positive energy.
   - You're ready to get started!

10
Thriving with Creativity

The central resource for a thriving life is *creativity*. Creativity comes from a place deep inside that springs up in the moment, unattached to thoughts of the past or future. Alive with the energy of *now*, creativity helps you discover unique solutions to your own distinct challenges. It also supports you in living in the present moment, which is more joyful and much richer.

Your new TAO is directly tied to your creativity because you are the architect and the artist in designing your life. You get to build and define it just the way you want to. Your creativity is the force behind the way you craft your new Take and select the Actions necessary to achieve how you want your life to look and be.

Creativity is a universal ability we all have that never goes away. It may be dormant at certain times, but it is there to serve you at every stage of your growth.

What exactly is creativity? Difficult to describe, it is like

- A lightbulb moment
- A flash of insight
- Divine inspiration

- A special battery power
- A force of nature
- A sudden burst of energy

Your creative spirit is often activated when you're searching for an answer or trying to communicate your ideas. Creativity is a process that breaks up standard assumptions and moves you to uncommon results. This process calls upon you to allow your spontaneous thoughts to surface.

Before we look at how you activate this gift, take some time to explore the issues, questions, and challenges that you may be faced with at this stage in your breakup and that can certainly be helped with creativity. After divorce or the breakup of a long-term relationship, you are essentially re-creating your identity and negotiating a new relationship with your former partner. In that process, you confront numerous decisions and opportunities. For example, you may be wrestling with where to settle, how to pursue your long-forgotten interests, where to work, or what your new life's purpose should be. All of these may be daunting issues until you realize that your creativity is there to assist you. So before we dive into how to access your creativity, take some time to define the questions to which you'd like answers.

Activate Your Creativity

One of the first tools at your disposal in activating creativity is the open-ended question. Questions with no preconceived "right" answers stimulate different parts of your brain and stir the imagination.

I once demonstrated this concept with a group of four-year-olds to an audience of teachers and administrators. Children, who are highly creative, are perfect messengers of just how effective a question with no "correct" answer can be. They illustrate how creativity comes naturally to us when we're young.

As I was telling the story of the Three Billy Goats Gruff, the children listened breathlessly, undistracted by being watched. I explained that the small, medium, and large goats wanted to cross a bridge to the other side of the river where the grass was greener. The problem was that a mean old troll lived under the bridge and wouldn't let them pass.

The smallest billy goat was tiptoeing lightly over the bridge when the troll rushed up to grab him. The little goat said, "You don't want me. Why don't you wait for my bigger brother?" The troll decided to wait.

The second billy goat also went gently over the bridge, but the troll heard him crossing and ran up. The middle-sized goat said, "Why don't you wait for my brother? He's much bigger than I am." And so the troll waited.

Big Billy Goat Gruff did not go quietly over the bridge. The troll dashed up and said, "I'm coming to get you now!" The big goat then lowered his enormous horns and knocked the troll into the river.

At this moment I stopped and asked, "What do you think happened to the troll?"

One eager child popped up and said, "You know . . . I think he floated on down the river . . . he crawled out in Ohio . . . and he's selling shoes at K-Mart."

Another child said, "The Pa-trol learned to swim . . . yeah . . . and I saw him at the swimming pool."

Another answer was, "My mommy dried him off, fed him dinner, and sent him home. He got in trouble when he got there."

All of the children's answers were imaginative and unique. Creativity is a gift we're all born with, but most of us have lost it in the course of life. In a supportive setting or as a result of learning to trust your own imagination, it can spring to life. When you learn to tap this inner resource, you'll begin to have a gusher of new ideas—not to mention being an inspiration to others.

Ideas for Unlocking Creativity

These are all tried-and-true techniques for unlocking your creativity. Experiment with them to see which ones work best for you.

Allow

You can allow the ideas to flow when you are alone, but you can also do it with people who are positive and supportive.

- Identify what you want.
- List your blocks to having what you want.
- Ask the open-ended question: what will it take to make it happen?
- Write all your ideas down or tape-record them as they come to you.
- Let them flow in a stream of consciousness.
- Don't judge your thoughts as they pour out.
- Continue to ask other questions, such as, "Whom can I talk to about this? Where can I create the help I need?"
- Read or listen to your ideas.
- Weed out the ones that don't quite work and make a short list of the ones that might.

You can address one issue at a time when you're brainstorming, but you will probably discover that eventually, your areas of concern overlap. For instance, the new job you find determines how much money you will earn, which affects where and how you will live. Creative ideas will help you tie these strands of thoughts together.

Brainstorming will bring you buckets of new ideas, and eventually you will find something in one of the buckets that will work for you.

Put yourself in a supportive environment

When you seek creativity, your soul calls for aesthetically pleasing surroundings that inspire and comfort you. When it comes to your work, seek situations where you can function with independence and be encouraged to take risks. You want to be in a place where you can't "fail." Positive, constructive feedback related to your ideas supports you in being even better at what you do. Situations where you can experiment, explore, and propose your concepts are where you will excel. Choose to be around people who are affirming and validating. Otherwise, your creativity will be stifled in an atmosphere of judgment, criticism, surveillance, or rigidity.

Listen to music

Music has the force to resonate in every part of you. Music can move, motivate, and carry you to places where you can let your mind drift. It brings you the chance to explore thoughts and feelings you didn't know you had, and can take you out of the ordinary and onto another plane. From that new place you can get new insights.

Keep recording materials nearby

Having a pen and notebook handy gives you the opportunity to jot down random ideas that may seem insignificant at the time but may mean something to you later. Writing tools can also help you capture a sudden resolution, a moment of inspiration, or another illuminating thought that you would lose if you did not put it on paper. Some people keep a laptop or a tape recorder nearby. Whatever works for you, do it. You can't keep everything in your head. When you need these ideas, you can access them if they're written down.

Do something physical

Take a walk, go to the gym, dance to music, ride a bike, or take a swim in order to activate other parts of your brain. Movement stimulates your body as well as your mind, and you need both for the growth of creativity. If you're stuck in a muddle of thoughts, get up and move.

Turn off the TV

Too much television numbs your senses, decreases your time for creative thought, and limits your interaction with others. If you turn it off, you will get inventive.

Rest

It's hard to come up with an original idea when you're tired. You need seven to eight hours of sleep each night, an occasional vacation from your work, and even a daily catnap. Creativity flows when you are rested.

If you are feeling flat, take a day off and get away from whatever you are working on. Don't go near your office or workspace. When you come back to it, you will feel refreshed and able to accomplish twice as much in half the time.

Hang out with other creative people

Sometimes when you are caught in your usual lines of thought, it can be hard to find new solutions. If you can't tap into your stream of ideas, look for other people who have it working for them and hang out together. People in the creative arts who have found positive ways to express themselves are good associations to make. Find some of them and begin a dialogue. Consider searching for a regular art night in your city or community; many creative people gather there.

Change your scenery

Even if you are not grappling with a problem, your creativity can still serve you in all aspects of life. But to keep that kind of energy flowing so that it's constantly available, you have to get out of the house. Go for a drive, visit a friend, take an overnight or weekend trip, and change what you see and do every day. Fresh new scenery visually stimulates your brain. If you can't get away, go for short walks in your neighborhood, taking a different route each time.

Change your habits

Just changing your seating position at the dinner table can give you a new perspective of the room, the other people, and the group dynamics. Changing habits can include driving to work on different roads or streets; going to another coffee shop for your morning cup of brew; and trying a different gas station, grocery store, or bakery. If you always drive, take a train, bus, trolley, or subway. Changing rituals and behaviors can give your brain a boost.

Give yourself parameters

Strangely enough, too much freedom limits creativity. In order for it to kick in, sometimes you need an assignment, a problem to solve, or a reason to express yourself. Occasionally, you need a smaller tool kit rather than a larger one.

To get started with the concept of working within limits, open a dictionary, randomly find a word, and write about your current situation incorporating this word. Or go outside, find one square foot of space, and write about it with descriptive words. At times, closing your eyes and visualizing your perfect getaway stimulates new thoughts.

Read, listen, and talk

Give your brain some exercise by reading, listening to someone else's innovative thoughts, and engaging in compelling conversations. Be diligent about maintaining the parts of your life that support these kinds of activities. Create a reading nook in your home that is quiet, comfortable, and well lit; attend lectures on subjects that might be out of your line of work but fascinate you; and find informed peers who challenge or contribute to your ideas.

Trust yourself

It's easy to think that someone else's answers are better than your own. When you are working with your creative flow, trust your inner voice, flashes of ideas, and knowledge of what is best for you. Also trust your recognition of the perfect books, mentors, or teachers appearing just when you need their wisdom. When you're searching for anything, stay alert to the surprising ways it can appear.

Sleep on it

Creativity is a process of conscious and unconscious insight. Before you fall asleep, pose your dilemma in your mind and ask for a resolution. Answers, associations, and concepts of originality and appropriateness can be generated while you sleep.

Incubate

The answers to the problem you are trying to solve may be internalized into your unconscious mind. If solutions are not forthcoming, you may need a period of incubation. Incubation is the time you give yourself to "forget" misleading clues or "logical" thinking. You need to remove yourself—mentally and emotionally—from the common assumptions about your personal issue that don't work for you before you become completely fixated on ineffective strategies. Be quiet, do something else to distract yourself, and give your ideas time to grow.

Many people who are in touch with their creativity know when it's time to incubate. Some head to their garden and get lost in hoeing and weeding. Others spend time hanging out with select friends, take long daily walks on the beach, or rock climb. My favorite time to incubate is while riding my quarter horse.

Try other creativity boosters

You want your creativity to serve you and bring out the best in your life. It's important to be aware of its power so that you don't misuse it. You want to understand how it works so that you can harness it. And you want to be able to recognize its qualities so that when the spark appears, you don't dismiss it. Pick two boosters from the following list to give this a try:

175

- Take a shower. Lots of great ideas can come to you then.
- Play with toys. Get down on the floor with a child, and play with him or her. Children's toys can stimulate your mind.
- Ask: What would my favorite person do? How would she solve this problem?
- Question yourself: What are my patterns from the past that were successful for me? What patterns did not work for me? How can I do things differently this time?

The Challenge for Ultra-Creatives

Just as some people may need help unlocking their creativity, others need help harnessing an abundance of creativity. My personal experience with educational systems, businesses, and coaching clients has led me to some observations on the characteristics of ultra-creative people. If you fall into this group, you may have come to see your creativity as a liability, because an abundance of it can pose challenges. Over your lifetime, you may have devalued your gift and stopped listening to your inner voice. But you can turn those challenges into opportunities, knowing that your creativity is your greatest asset for surviving and thriving.

For starters, creative people may not always perform well on tests because they are not concerned with test performance, proving their intelligence, or getting all the answers right. They aren't necessarily trying to be rebellious in test situations; it's just that their creativity can lead them astray. The creative person may try to comply with the rules and stick to the time limits, especially with IQ tests, but if one question captures her imagination, she will "forfeit" a good score to let her mind wander to whimsical, offbeat solutions.

If you've ever worried that your IQ score was not as high as you'd thought it should be, perhaps this is one reason why: you're creative. If you've let the thought that you weren't smart enough hold you back, now you can let go of it.

In addition, creative people often care what only a few select people think of their performance or their work. Their spirits can rise and fall (especially when they're young) according to how these people react, and they aren't that concerned about what the rest of the world thinks. If this sounds like you, the good news is that you are now at an age where you can consciously choose new mentors and important people in your life. Select those who are encouraging, helpful, and wise.

Also, intensely creative people must have an outlet for their imaginations or they will create drama. If they can't find a positive way to express their ideas, the whole world becomes a stage for acting out one crisis after another. Creative people are natural-born problem solvers and must have constructive challenges to work out.

Creative people can experience emotional highs and lows as they struggle to

- Find a problem to solve
- Look for the answer
- Have their "aha" moment
- Not grow bored with a project before it's finished
- Look for their next challenge
- Be patient with those who don't understand them

If these characteristics sound like yours, you may be an ultra-creative. The good news is that you have the potential to enrich your own life and the world. But you need an outlet for all that creative energy. The best way to harness your creative power is to redirect it toward solving something that brings you happiness, vigor, fortune, and health. What is that outlet for you?

My client Electra struggled with mastering her gift of creativity. She was funny, she was inventive, and she was confused about her life. Married for fifteen years with no children, Electra and Blake had separated three times and then gotten back together. Electra said she never felt the kind of passion for Blake that she wished she could, and after years of counseling, they got divorced. She came to see me after they had been divorced for three years and she was searching for a career.

Electra had multiple interests but had never finished her degree because she kept changing her major. She was a rabbit chaser: if something came hopping by, she stopped what she was doing and went chasing after it. She wrote poetry, was politically active in conservation, and loved anthropology. She had been the contractor on several houses she and Blake had built together. Not only was she enthusiastic about a lot of subjects, but she was also gifted at whatever she did.

What originally attracted Electra and her husband to each other eventually caused their breakup. She was drawn to his stability; he was attracted to her artistic and spontaneous nature. Their initial interpretations of each other shifted to his being rigid and narrow-minded and her being flighty and irresponsible. They both felt misunderstood and unappreciated. The last time they broke up, they knew they would never again be able to live together.

Electra lacked a focus and a plan for her life. The constancy her husband had provided by having a routine was gone. When she came to see me, the simple but central question I posed to her was, What do you want? True to her deeply creative nature, she was all over the map.

While Electra was talking, I could not help but marvel at how engaging she was. It was as easy to get caught up in her web of ideas as it was for her to drift off into them, with no practical plan of how to structure her life. She was warm and funny and lovely—with an obvious longing for direction just under the surface of her chatter.

"There are so many things I would like to do," she said. "I want to write books and make a contribution to the world."

I said, "Let's start with a vision for your life. How about writing out a plan for the next year, the next five years, and the next ten years? Where do you want to be and what do you want to be doing?"

Electra and I worked for months on her career plan and goals. This was difficult for her because until she got some clarity, she would change it every other day.

Pinning down exactly what to do and when to do it is counter-intuitive for so many creative people. But without a plan, they can dash from interest to interest, giving each one momentary heat and then turning cold and moving on. Focusing on how to weave critical interests and talents together while leaving a little room for important hobbies is one of their biggest obstacles. They get distracted from their goals when they have too many projects going on.

Each week, we came back to the question, What do you want? Finally, she was ready to make a commitment to herself. She said, "I'm sure now that I want to express myself, and through that expression, I want to serve others. I'm getting an idea of what medium to choose, but I need more financial security under me so I can go to school."

"How can you accomplish this?" I asked. "Whom could you ask to give you some direction?"

Electra went to Blake, who was an investment broker, and asked for his help in laying out her future finances. With his advice, she discovered that if she sold her house and combined the proceeds with the money she had left, she would have enough to put aside and live off the interest. Blake helped her with the sale of the house and showed her how to set up an account that would pay a monthly dividend. He also helped her move into a small cottage on a wooded hillside. She was extremely grateful for his guidance as well as his time and expertise.

Electra's plan for her new life is to become a writer. She is taking classes in journalism and attending writers' conferences. Recently she had an article published in a national magazine, and she has begun to write a nature column for her local newspaper. She has an agreement with herself to spend the morning hours writing and the afternoons studying. Electra has found a mentor to help her stay on track. If a new interest captures her attention, she writes down her ideas and information about it and files them away, knowing that some of them may get incorporated into her books.

Electra knows that she can become a hostage to her creativity, all tied up in knots and unable to make a decision about what to do. She watches her inclination to run after new fascinations closely and channels her constant curiosity into actions for her work.

Blake and Electra talked frequently for a while. She said they fell out of love years ago, but after discovering how to have kinder conversations, they fell "in like." He remarried last year, and Electra is happy for him and will never forget how he helped her get on her path.

Electra had the problem of struggling to harness her creativity. Many people, however, are often stuck in only being able to see one way to do something. They keep doing the same things over and over and getting the same results. This is a common problem clients bring to coaches. The best way to get unstuck is through tapping your creative energy. If this is what you need, try the suggestions in "Ideas for Unlocking Creativity" on pages 170–176.

Do not underestimate the power of creativity. Using it will reward you with energy and accomplishments, because creativity is where your answers are. It helps you be more resilient, make the necessary changes in your life, and find new doors that will open for you. When times get hard, creative people are the ones who survive by adapting. They reinvent themselves, they figure out what needs to be done, and they do it.

Creativity can help you make the most of this time in your life. Knowing that you will never have a challenge without being able to find the solution is liberating . . . as well as exhilarating.

Creativity can give you choices, it can shine up your confidence, and it can provide you with the ability to design a better way to be a better friend—to yourself and to those around you. Just imagine the possibilities.

Suggestions for Enhancing Your Creative Power

1. **Let the ideas flow.**
   With your journal or notebook, follow the sequence of activities in the "Allow" section on pages 170–171. Be sure to answer the open-ended questions.

2. **Remember.**
   What was your favorite creative activity as a child?
   When were you most creative as an adult and what were you doing?
   What unique solutions have you come up with in your life and how did they serve you?

3. **Write your reflections.**

What did your life look like a year ago?

What does it look like now?

Where do you want to be in one year? Five years? Ten years? Get creative!

4. **Use a tape recorder.**

Visualize your current challenge. Close your eyes and let your thoughts flow on this subject. Use vivid, descriptive words to talk about

- What you see
- What you hear
- What you can touch
- What you smell
- What you can taste
- What you feel

What are some of the solutions for your situation? In stream-of-consciousness style, talk it out.

Listen to all the above and write down the useful points.

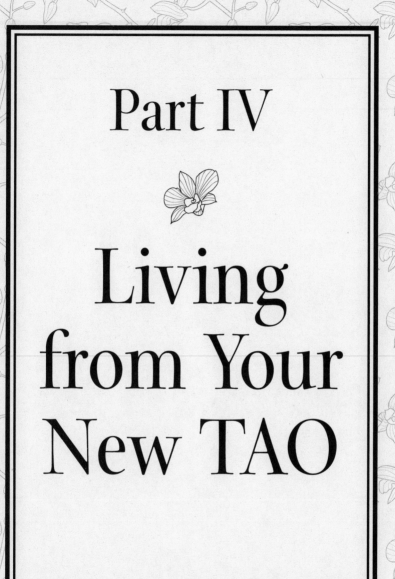

Part IV

Living from Your New TAO

11
Considering
New Relationships

As you move forward living from your new TAO, the perspective you've found along your journey will bring your life vibrancy, color, harmony, and depth. This is the new you—and you're shining.

You have now experienced what happens when you rewrite the negative script that used to play in your thoughts and crystallize in your words. With a positive Take, your Actions become the means to reaching a changed, superior Outcome.

Just as you have crafted a different relationship with your ex, you may now want to reexamine your other friendships and connections. It's possible to create better bonds with family members and old friends. Existing relationships can become like new ones because, truly, people treat you the way you treat yourself. As you rise to a higher level of self-regard, those around you will shift their opinions and behaviors.

For those who might be invested in your staying limited in the scope of your life, you may need more solid boundaries or greater emotional distance. You're strong enough to handle this now. When you give your life greater relevance, you have an impetus to honor who you are and who you continue to become.

Now that you are living from your new TAO, where do you go from here? You are ready to look at a stronger definition of friendship. You need people in your corner who support your new actions, attitudes, and dreams. Since this is your new life, you want to carefully select who gets to share it. You may even want to start dating.

As you get into different friendships and straighten out old ones, it helps to have some criteria with which to identify healthy, supportive relationships—the kind of qualities that align with you in your new state of being.

Communication

You now want friends you can *communicate* with. When you talk, do they listen? When they speak, do you love to hear what they have to say? When they reflect on what you've said, rather than pushing their own agenda, do they return your ideas with value added? You treasure friends who contribute to your growth by sharing what they have learned from their life's lessons.

Understanding each other is key. Consider the parallel of foreign travel: your biggest obstacle in a new country is communication. Where you go, how you get there, the exchange of money, and how to interact in a different culture can all be huge challenges. The possibility of seeming rude or ignorant is enormous and can lead to unfortunate consequences. A mutual understanding can be critical to the success of your visit—and, sometimes, to your survival.

This example holds true in all types of relationships. If you aren't speaking each other's "language," understanding needs and requests, sharing the same humor, or grasping each other's values, misunderstandings can occur. At this stage along your TAO, easy communication is the essence of your new relationships.

Positive Energy

Listen carefully when your friend talks. Does the person always have a problem that is not her fault, consumes her thoughts day and night, and is the reason she can never be happy? Or is he bitter, angry, and argumentative? This is an example of what can happen to a dear friend who is going through a divorce. Such reactions and behavior can be hard to be around; if this is someone you care about, you could recommend that he or she see a counselor or coach.

Some people never show any desire to find answers, look for hope, or seek insight, whether they are going through a divorce or dealing with any other kind of challenging issue. When you are around these people, you need to guard your heart, your time, and the energy required to interact with them. You need your energy to take care of your life. Protect what you are building, which is your place in the world that has meaning and gives you pride and comfort. Likewise, be aware of the messages you send.

Conversations of Substance and Hope

When you are living your new TAO, your conversations take on added significance in thought and meaning. You are more in touch with yourself, aware of your strengths, and confident from your successes. You now know how to extend encouragement to others and are alert to the fact that a negative focus only grows more negativity. You pay attention to what others think and say. They may unconsciously be looking for comfort or agreement on life's problems, but you find their positive core, recognizing the heart of each person. Your life and conversations are examples of hope to others, which offer the positive side of situations.

Telegraphing Confidence

People with confidence are present and accessible. When you are with others, you telegraph to them what you think of yourself and they send that opinion back to you. When you are aligned with your thoughts, words, feelings, and deeds, you are enough, just as you are ... and that's what you convey to others. That's why everyone wants to be near you.

Alive with Authenticity

As an authentic person, you wouldn't know how to be anyone else but yourself, nor would you want to be. You enjoy your friends, welcome meeting new people, throw your arms around your work, and never fear being alone. You have learned to like your own company. You are always growing and learning, and from season to season, your integrity is your rock. Whatever you are doing, it is stamped with your authentic mark.

Standards

You are becoming aware of a greater force pulling you to your higher calling. You have longed for this feeling in the past but you didn't know how to get there. Now you trust where your life is leading you. Where you are heading may not be familiar territory, but it's where your spiritual self wants to be and why you are using your divorce for growth. In building new friendships, you remember your list of values. They guide you toward making better choices. You'll feel a kindred spirit with other people working toward similar goals or with those who already reached theirs.

These are the qualities that sustain you as you attract new friendships of depth.

Preparing for New Friendships

When you embrace your new TAO, you have greater reverence for your life. It is clear that what you think and say, the actions you take, and the outcomes you receive are inextricably woven together and enormously significant. You strive to stay in this consciousness to sustain your continuing growth and empowerment. More than ever, now is the time to remember these points:

Slow down

Your feet may want to run faster and faster toward your exciting new life, but to maintain your dignity and elegance, take time to find your new stride. Since you aren't being defined by your partnership any longer, this is your moment to relax into your unique self. Move to a slower beat, keeping the pace liquid and serene. Just say no to rushing and too many deadlines, emails, phone calls, appointments, messages, and meetings. As you give up living life from crisis to crisis, you feel rested, prepared, and even younger.

How do you do this?

- Get your work done well before deadlines so you lessen your stress.
- Let your voice mail take the messages and call people back on your schedule. (You especially don't need to field personal calls when you are emotionally tired.)
- Let go of people who drag you down, sap your energy, and take you into old, unproductive (or destructive) habits.
- Don't overcommit to anything.
- Take some classes in yoga and meditation and practice deep breathing, which can lower your heart rate and blood pressure.

Banish worry from your life

Whenever you fret, consciously change your focus from whatever you are obsessing about and instead wrap yourself around today. Worrying brings you fear of your tomorrows. If you spend the day doing the best job you can and make realistic, productive plans for your future, you're doing a good job. You now know that whatever you focus on is what you grow more of. Remember to put your concentration on the positive.

Give and receive generously

It's a mature person who can receive compliments and gifts with a smile and a warm thank-you. You can now allow yourself to be big enough to feel you deserve them. If small or even lavish gifts make you squirm or sincere praise makes you fidget or feel uncomfortable, ask yourself what you need to forgive yourself for. This is the time to clear up any lingering doubts about anything—because you deserve all that you've worked for.

Acknowledge your wins

It's just amazing how some people never stop to allow an enormous accomplishment to sink in. Instead of hugging themselves (metaphorically) and saying, "Well done!" they are already off and planning their next big project without taking a breath. If you do that long enough, you will begin to feel like you are on an unending treadmill of performance. That gets exhausting.

Take a look at what you have become good at, your successes, and your symbolic or real badges of merit. You've earned them, and acknowledgment is warranted. Shine a beam of light on all the good you do, and more good will come back to you.

Focus on what you are grateful for every day

Do you have trouble with this suggestion? If you don't know where to start, turn on a news channel and take a look at what the vast majority of people live with—and without—all the time.

To build your attitude of gratitude, start with appreciating the smallest things—the way the sunlight streams through your windows, the trees along your street or in the park, the constantly changing picture in the sky. Remember your best teachers, your favorite neighbors or relatives, and your best friends. Keep going down the list of what you treasure.

Why is this little exercise important? Because when you live with this grateful attitude, it is very difficult to be angry with anyone or to look at the world through a lens of lack.

Build a new social life

Has it been a long time since you have gone to parties, picnics, dances, or celebrations? Would you like to start going out more often and meeting new people?

Interacting socially is good for you. It gives you practice with a different level of conversation, it helps you relate gracefully to others in your work, and it helps you find new friends. An appropriately active social life can introduce you to new activities, new people, and even new dates.

Thinking about Dating

Are you at a point where you would like to consider dating? Has it been a long time? Would you like to learn how to become successful at meeting people you can go out with? If so, maybe you need a plan.

We usually plan for everything else in life. We have financial plans, health plans, educational plans, and even travel plans. But not too many people have a focused dating plan. Why?

Most of us don't think we need it. We usually wait to see what comes our way and then react. If we don't like what we see, we continue to wait and watch. Somehow, we don't think we should have to do any work for a date. We think it should just "happen."

One of my clients, Terry, had been on a career track all his life. His parents sent him to the best schools, and his summers were planned with camp, travel, and sports. His after-school programs were strictly monitored, with activities planned to further his growth and career.

Terry has a good job and some friends he met in high school and college, and he would like to date more. Does he have a plan? No. He goes out every weekend to the same places, barely looks up from his beer to see who is there, and talks about how there isn't anyone to meet in this town.

Why doesn't Terry have a plan? He has one for everything else in his life. Isn't meeting someone to date and possibly have a relationship with just as important?

When Terry understood that *he* had to do some work to meet people, we looked at where he would start. He first had to get clear about what kinds of people he wanted to date.

If you're like Terry, here is a place for you to begin. Ask yourself the following questions and pay attention to your answers. They could change your life.

1. **What am I looking for?**
   Don't rush this question. Sit down and start to write out the qualities that are important to you. Make an actual wish list on paper. Many people choose dates based on how the person looks and whether he or she shares some similar interests. Though it is true that chemistry is important, there is much more that needs to be considered. Ultimately, you're looking to see if the other person has the values you can't live without.

2. **What am I willing to do to get what I want?**
   You can say you want something, but how committed are you to it? What action are you willing to take to make it happen? Have you worked hard to have the career you have today? Realize that it might take that same kind of commitment to alter your current habits of socializing if you want to meet new people.

3. **What is the most important thing I could do to create results?**
   Are you willing to step out of familiar (but ineffective) behaviors and try something new? Are you ready to take some risks, like asking people to fix you up? Can you go to new places and reach out to people? A different Take and different Actions are now required to get a different Outcome.

4. **How can I use a recent experience to avoid mistakes in the future?**
   Most of us are doomed to repeat the same errors over and over unless we stop and look at our patterns of behavior. This

is uncomfortable. Take a look at your failed dating experiences and ask yourself what your Take was then and how you acted it out. How can you use the experience gained from your breakup for more dating and relationship wisdom?

5. **How can I face the prospect of dating with a positive attitude?**
   If we take responsibility for the challenges in our lives and don't blame others for them, we can spend our energy looking for solutions. With this attitude, you can also take responsibility for finding the kinds of dates you want. You can do this now because you understand how the TAO can work for you.

When you spend some time answering these questions, you'll be ready to think about a plan.

How to Start Dating

Day after day, I hear hundreds of reasons why people don't date. Their explanations start with, "I can't get a date because . . ."

- My mother is Russian and I learned to be cold from her.
- I've tried every book and counselor I could find, and nothing works for me.
- Nothing gives me energy, so I'm unattractive.
- The only person I've ever loved married someone else ten years ago.
- I'm forty-five and have never been married, and the odds of my finding someone are zero.
- I'm fifty-six and married and divorced five times; who would want to date me?

- There's no one out there; everyone is married or gay.

The truth is, these people can't get a date because of their Take. If you share similar thoughts, think about the following:

Plan #1: Shift the myth of *rejection*

Start by examining your inner voice. A negative Take could be holding you back. Thinking you can be "rejected" is an insidious condition that's as disabling as any disease. It thwarts your actions, subverts your good intentions, and holds you hostage to a meager perspective. So many great people never have a dating life because they are afraid of being rejected.

Then they accumulate more and more "proof" that they are not datable or lovable. The "proof," of course, comes from their negative Take, which produces Actions that don't bring results. When you gather biased evidence, you either settle for someone you don't really want, or you don't go out at all because you think someone might not want you.

Letting go of the idea of rejection will set you free. Once you understand that you have the power over how you feel and think about yourself, no one can "reject" you. If someone indicates she doesn't want to go out with you, this is helpful information. You don't want to go out with her. Strong self-esteem dictates that you don't want to date people who don't appreciate you, see you, or feel the magic.

It's also easy to misunderstand someone's lack of social skills. I have seen many shy or insecure people who aren't very talkative, don't open up, appear unfriendly, and, therefore, send potential dates away. If you or the person you are talking to exhibits these traits, know that we all think we have been rejected when we are in the company of seemingly aloof behavior.

Accepting the concept of rejection, believing the false evidence of not being worthy of attracting dates, and being thwarted by a lack of social skills all need to be addressed if you want to start dating. With your new life on track and with all you have learned from your former relationships and your divorce, you can get past any of these blockages. You've got the tools to do it now.

Plan #2: *Do* something to get dates

If you feel you are ready to date, have your life reasonably aligned, and have taken time to discover who you are after breaking up with your ex, it's probably time for you to get moving. Lots of dates are waiting to meet you. What you can't do is sit in front of the TV and expect the dating world to arrive.

If you only get out once in a while, your chances of meeting someone are slim. Attending the annual holiday party or going to your class reunion is better than going nowhere at all, but if this is all you do, you are probably going to go home—alone—and feel rejected. A few actions do not usually equal success.

When you focus on meeting lots of people and when you are friendly, you already have a better-than-average chance of dating. Clearly, the next step is to take some new Actions.

Here are some techniques and tips to help you meet someone:

Try the internet

The internet has brought many people together. Browse some dating sites and then sign up with one that feels right to you. Sites that charge a fee to join are usually safer and better than free sites.

Yes, you have to use caution, just as you would in meeting any stranger anywhere. Start out following these tips and eventually you will become savvy about who is appropriate and who isn't: never loan anyone money, do not give out your home phone number or address, use an untraceable cell phone for initial calls, and exit the conversation if the person makes any type of inappropriate sexual comments.

The best approach to attracting dates through this venue is to write an interesting profile. If you aren't good at describing yourself and your interests, ask a friend for help. Avoid using clichés such as how you like "candlelight dinners and walking on the beach." Though you may love those two things, so does everyone else. The point is to have your personality shine through while talking about what is unique to your life.

Did you vindicate yourself by winning the swing dance contest in junior high, right after you lost the spelling bee? Are you fond of growing worms in the greenhouse you built? Did you once have a potbellied pig named Myrna for a pet? These are some of the comments that will make you memorable among many other profiles.

Post recent *flattering* pictures of yourself. Some of the photos I've seen on dating sites looked like they came straight from people's driver's licenses. We all know how scary that can be. Other people posted twenty-year-old photos. The last thing you need is for your date to be disappointed upon your meeting because he or she thought you were a much younger person.

Don't wait a long time to meet someone you could be interested in. You won't know if the chemistry is there until you have a face-to-face conversation. Here are some precautions to take for a first meeting: Start out by having a coffee date. Use your own transportation to get there. Never have your date drive you home until you know each other well. Tell friends where you're going, and if one wants to be an anonymous person in the coffee shop, that's even better. If you think you want to see the person again, you can always get a background check to find out if he's trustworthy.

I have a sixty-nine-year-old client who races home from her business every day to see who has contacted her on the internet. Men are flying in from other states, and even countries, to take her out. She's having a ball, and so can you.

Ask for introductions

Your friends want to support you. You can let go of any embarrassment in asking them introduce you to someone. This is not beneath you—it's smart. Ask people if they know anyone who is interesting and single. Ask them more than once, and ask more than one person.

Put yourself in social settings

Look at your community's calendar of events in the newspaper. Check out the gatherings within your spiritual group or with the hobbies you love. Conferences, seminars, lectures, conventions, and trade shows are all possible places to meet people. And don't forget singles events.

Activities in all these areas are usually planned in advance, so make an agreement with a friend to go together. If you can't get anyone to go with you, go by yourself. Knock yourself out being friendly when you get there, and do the following:

1. **Do a scan.** When you get to where you're going, scan the room to see if there is someone you want to meet. If you don't see anyone who looks dateable, talk to the friendliest person in the room to keep building your social skills. Use every opportunity to make new friends. *Do not* sit down and hope someone finds you.

2. **Position yourself.** Stand near an entrance, refreshment area, aisle, or water fountain. If you go with friends, unhook from them at some point and stand alone. Be accessible and approachable. I've heard people say they saw someone they wanted to meet, but the person was in a booth with four friends. They couldn't get near the person and there were too many people listening if they had tried to talk.

3. **Enter the zone.** If you see someone interesting, move within talking distance and make a friendly comment. This is a critical time, from "entering the zone" to "closing" the conversation. If you get interrupted at any point, statistics have shown that it is unlikely you will get a chance to pick up the thread and complete the encounter, so be focused.

4. **Think of wearing or carrying something that is a conversation starter.** When you're out in public venues, carry a book, tennis racquet, guitar, or even an empty birdcage. Wear a hat with a logo. Wear a shirt with the name of your college. These should not just be props but something that is authentic to you. The point is to don an accessory that encourages people to talk to you and makes it easier for them to be friendly and ask questions.

   I once had a lapel button that read, "My Mother Is a Rodeo Queen." It had a picture of my mother racing her horse. It always initiated questions. I also carried my autoharp through airports when I was on my way to give a concert— I couldn't walk ten feet without someone asking about it.

5. **Share something (vaguely) personal.** In conversation, say something that reveals who you are or what you are interested in, but keep it generic. For example, "Before I came tonight,

I had to ____" (feed my hedgehog; blanket my horse; water my basil and thyme; and so on). Statements like this help initiate questions and comments.

6. **Resist wearing a ring on any finger.** When people are looking at you from across a crowded room, they can't tell which finger your ring is on. They may mistake it for a wedding ring and, therefore, not approach you.

    Also, don't wear a headset in the gym or when you're out jogging. People can't talk to you if you do.

Plan #3: Seize the moment

Once you start having a conversation, this is your chance to see if you want to date this person. Make sure you get his name and where he works early in the conversation, in case you get interrupted. If your meeting was cut short and you felt there was some chemistry and interest between you, you can call him or her at work and say, "This is Mary Doe. I met you at the such and such event the other night," to see if you can continue talking. If he doesn't respond positively, let it go. But it's always worth one call to find out if there's a possible connection.

Plan #4: Closing the conversation

If you want to get to know the person better, suggest an activity and give the person your private cell number or email address, or even ask him or her to coffee. (Having coffee with someone is not considered a date; it is where you decide if you want to have a date in the future.) If the person is vague about meeting up with you, move on. There are other dating possibilities just around the corner.

Sending Dating Signals

Letting people know you are interested in them requires that you send out signals. Transmitting nonverbal cues is the way to tell someone you'd like to talk, which could lead to a date. When you talk, you get to see if you are attracted to him or her. It is then that you decide if you want to go out with this person. This kind of conversation is like dancing: see if you are in sync, don't step on each other's toes, and see if it flows.

What exactly do the dating signals look like?

Smile

This is the universal signal in every culture that tells people you like something about them. It's often an invitation that says, "Come closer." If both people smile at each other, a connection has begun. A smile speaks volumes—from across a crowded room or face-to-face in a conversation. An attractive smile is your greatest asset, so check your teeth after you eat a salad or spinach or olives. A big splash of green or black on your front tooth can throw people off balance; they don't quite know what to say to you.

Eye Contact

Communicating your interest in someone becomes more compelling with eye contact. Some people can't help but feel drawn to a person who holds their gaze. To enhance the possibility of attracting someone you are interested in, wear an accessory or piece of clothing that is the exact color of your eyes, and wear it near your face. If your eyes are blue and your shirt is the same color of blue, it's hard for anyone to turn away from you. Ditto for brown or green eyes.

You also might try the complete-eye-contact technique. Here are the steps:

- Make friendly eye contact that lasts just a little longer than is comfortable.
- Drop your eyes when you see you have connected.
- Look back up and gaze a little longer, with the hint of a smile.

Talking

Once you have made the eye contact and the smile connection and you want to start a conversation, try not to get sidelined as you move toward the object of your intention. If you stop to talk to other people, it is very hard, if not impossible, to pick up the thread of energy that has been started.

Don't be put off if he or she isn't moving toward you. Many people are shy and will stand there, frozen, hoping you will send more signals. When you are near enough to talk, ask a question:

Are you from this town?

Have you been here before?

Where did you grow up?

These three questions should lead to more questions and answers. After a few minutes into this conversation, you'll know if you want to continue.

If you are attracted to the person and he or she isn't saying much but is smiling and blushing, keep talking until the shyness melts. But if he or she is cold, distant, or rude, move away and look for other people to meet. Don't waste time with anyone who is not kind or friendly. You have nothing to prove.

The Arm Touch

If your conversation is going well, there is nothing quite as effective in letting people know you like them as a spontaneous touch on the arm. If you laugh easily, reach out and touch the person's forearm, hand, or shoulder. That touch releases the tension between two people who are feeling drawn to each other. The gesture should be totally natural, just as it would be with any other friend. If you don't know how to do this, start practicing on old friends or family members.

The first conversation is also an opportunity to find out if this person meets some of your requirements. Ask questions about topics important to you or make comments on those subjects to get a reaction. (For example, If you are passionate about animals, mention an article you'd just read in a magazine and watch the response.)

The art of conversation can be used in any setting. In the dating world, reaching out to others is the way you communicate that you might like to know someone better. But when you are out meeting people, who can get to know you if you don't talk or if you mumble or give abrupt answers?

Josh wanted to meet someone and finally got up the courage to go to a singles event. Before he went, we practiced what he would say when he introduced himself. I told him, "Pretend you are talking to someone you are meeting for the first time. What would you say?" He drew a blank. He said, "I can't think of anything."

"Josh, you are a very sweet guy, and anyone would be happy to know you. I know you can find something to say that will give people a chance to talk with you. We just need to think about it, bring it up, and practice.

"I'll demonstrate: 'Hi, I'm Tonja. I'm a coach and a columnist. I got here late tonight. Have I missed anything so far? I was late because I took my three-legged dog for a walk. She got tired and sat down on the sidewalk, and I had to carry her home. She weighs about fifty pounds. Next time I walk her, I'll take a wagon.'"

What was the point of that introduction? You want to give the other person enough information to

- Ask you questions.
- Feel comfortable talking to you.
- Know something personal but benign about your life so he or she has some inkling as to who you are.

Also, everyone likes to be around friendly people who talk and answer questions with more than one-word answers.

Then it was Josh's turn. He mumbled in a voice I could barely hear, "Hi, I'm Josh." At this point, he rolled his eyes, like what he was about to say was embarrassing, and said, "I'm from *Ohio.*"

Obviously, we had to get more creative. We finally got his introduction more upbeat.

Here are some tips that apply to everyone:

Use a voice that can be heard and understood

Being shy can be endearing, but if no one can hear you, how can they be charmed? This was Josh's problem. If he did speak, the volume was below anyone's range of hearing. If you are in a large room with lots of ambient noise and people talking, you can't be understood if you mumble or your voice is too soft.

Be proud of where you're from

What's the problem with Ohio? It's a lovely state, and any place is a good place if you came from there. Be proud of your history and your family—even if they're from Oz. That just makes you interesting. Stay focused on your other good qualities too.

Keep your sharing appropriate

You don't want to give people more information than they can handle. Share your personal problems and challenging moments when you know others well and you trust them. By this time in your life, you want to have your baggage unpacked and be traveling light when you're out meeting people.

Tell a funny story about yourself

Laughing with someone builds a bond toward friendship. Politicians, attorneys, judges, corporate leaders, and even media stars seek coaching in the art of telling a story. They know the power of making people laugh. Stay away from a story that might be construed as making fun of someone else. You don't want to sound mean. Telling something about yourself that reveals your human side can be refreshing.

Why is this important in dating? It's easy to forget a name or even a face if you meet a lot of people at once. But you won't forget a funny story.

Someone sat next to me at a wedding reception ten years ago, and I still remember her. She told me she had a problem with her dog, a cocker spaniel that was wearing her patience thin. It seems that every time the doorbell rang, the dog got confused, started barking, and *bit* her. Stories like that just stay with a person.

Dating New People

If you want to avoid some of the longest hours of your life, counting the seconds until you can gracefully exit a date, remember some of these stories and tips:

Tip #1: Keep the first date short

A Shakespearean actress I coach, Zoe, met someone on the internet. She liked the music he said he listened to, so she thought he sounded like a match—until he drove up to her desert town in his rusty pickup truck with no air conditioning in July. In 110-degree heat, sweat melting her makeup, they drove off for a *day* of adventure.

He drove her to a small lake to go fishing in a (rocking) tiny rowboat. She was nervous . . . and sweltering. Then they headed to a truck stop for hamburgers and fries. Finally, he drove her home, which took three hours in traffic. She said the only adventure she had that day was trying to make conversation after the first hour of the date . . . and catching her false eyelashes as they melted in the heat and fell off.

Another client, Matt, was asked to dinner at the home of his blind date. He imagined a lovely evening of getting to know her over a home-cooked meal. When he drove up, he noticed that the mailbox had a cat painted on it, but he didn't pick up on the clue.

She opened the door, smiling and brushing cats away from her feet. Inside, cats were *everywhere*—clawing the furniture, eating off dirty dishes in the sink, and lying on thick layers of cat hair on the carpet. He said the smell from the litter boxes almost put him in a coma.

He began to sneeze before cocktails. Cats were on his shoulders, rubbing against his ankles, and crawling into his lap. During the first course, his eyes were running like flowing tears, and he was beginning to have trouble breathing. He apologized profusely and said he had to leave because he had forgotten his allergy medicine. He sped away, not looking back, for fear the cats were chasing him.

Not everyone requires a date to have an air-conditioned truck in the desert, and some people don't mind a house with lots of cats. But most people need to know these things before they plan to spend a *whole day* or a long evening with someone. These are the kinds of innocent mistakes you don't need to make. Here are a couple of tips:

- Meet on neutral territory in a public place and drive yourself there. Then you'll know if you want to see more of each other. If it's not working, you can excuse yourself early.
- Dinner dates can be complicated. Trying to eat a meal while you get to know someone for the first time can be awkward. Instead, try a walk or a visit to the aquarium. And if you focus on getting to know each other first and you happen to like each other, you may not *care* about a lack of air conditioning or an abundance of cat hair. It might not be a problem at all.

Tip #2: Bring yourself

Nothing is harder on two people—you and your date—than one person showing up but not really being there. If your mind and heart are lost in the past or you are internally fussing about your future and what "might happen," you are not available. You might be doing this because you are nervous. It happens.

If you have trouble staying in the present, anchor yourself with something you notice in the current setting that has a scent or texture or a particular presence. For instance, perhaps the coffee shop has a strong aroma of coffee beans. Focus on that smell as you begin your conversation. If your mind is thinking about the dry cleaning you have to drop off or the last conversation you had with your ex, your date will never get to meet you.

Tip #3: Keep your boundaries in mind

Remembering your boundaries is the key to enjoying any date. Did you know that objects in nature that do not have distinct boundaries become invisible? You don't want to be barely visible in the world.

Be clear in your own mind about what you want to do and what you don't. Don't complicate the situation by making apologies or excuses. Simply communicate your boundaries whenever necessary in a kind way. Knowing you are in control of your decisions and choices will help you be calm and confident.

Tip #4: Find your safe place

Dating someone new can sometimes make you feel anxious, self-conscious, or insecure. When those emotions take over, you need a safe place to go to. Where would that be? Go inside your own mind. Visualize yourself on your favorite beach or mountaintop or visiting your grandmother. Surround yourself with the feelings you have when you're there, and then return to the present, relaxed. Along your TAO, you've learned to transform Takes and Actions, so rely on this skill whenever you need to.

Rephrase any negative thought into one that is positive, such as turning "I look like a mess today" into "I look just perfect, and when I smile at people, they smile back." It's simple, and, honestly, it works.

Tip #5: Look for something good about your date

If you know your boundaries, you will be relaxed enough to look for the good in your date. Whether you hit it off or not, you can still find something real or terribly human that you appreciate. When you do, compliment what you see. Often, when two people aren't suited for each other, they walk away feeling compelled to list the other person's faults. But you'll feel better about yourself and the world when you focus on something that's right about your date—even if you are not interested in seeing each other again.

In this stage of your divorce, you will have mastered the art of kindness, civility, and the ability to see the divinity in everyone. With that new ability, you attract others easily, make new friends, and even find the time to consider dating.

All your special qualities, polished and shining, are the gifts from what you have learned. Quietly say a prayer of thanks for everything you've gone through.

Suggestions for Building Your New Relationships

1. **Planning with friends**
   Write your social appointments on your calendar. Consider allotting a minimum of seven hours a week for interacting with friends. Call and ask friends to join you for the following activities:

   - Brunch, lunch, or dinner
   - A fun activity
   - Exercise or sports
   - Concerts, lectures, or classes

2. **Dating plans**

Write on your calendar your plans for meeting potential dates:

- Name of event or activity
- Location
- Day and time
- Whom I will go with
- What I will wear
- Other planning details for this event

3. **Practice**

Before you go places to socialize and meet new people, practice how you will deliver

- An introduction of who you are
- Your short personal history
- A funny story about yourself

12
Defining Your Legacy

It has been said that life is a journey and not just a destination; the future you intend is coming to fruition with each step you take. Of course, you will continue to face the trying events that all people experience, but you will have the confidence and resilience to get through them with grace. As you live your new TAO of Divorce and incorporate this new way of being into your daily life, you have the tools to deal calmly and carefully with nearly any relationship challenge that comes your way. You not only learn from life's adversities or uncertainties, you thrive!

Living your new TAO also means you have made a shift from your former perceptions to a more enlightened, positive look at what your breakup, divorce, or separation means for your future. It doesn't have to define you, but as you've seen and learned throughout this book, the strength you've gained has changed you. You've passed through the trials this transition has brought you and come out the other side as a new, stronger person. You have expanded your consciousness, as well as your ability to relate to everyone, by reaching for the insights during this passage. Without giving in to any oppositions along your path, you have learned to flow effortlessly around or over them. Congratulations!

Shining a Light

If you were to look back to before you shifted your TAO, would you recognize yourself? It's likely that your changes haven't gone unnoticed by those around you. Your example has the potential to be a beacon of hope to others.

Several years after my divorce, I received a letter from a neighbor. She was one of the young, attractive women in my daughter's nursery school carpool group. She was married to a doctor and had a gorgeous house and two beautiful children. I remember feeling poor and pitiful as I pulled up in her driveway twice a week and she put her child in my old car. During that year, we never said more than hello to each other, but from where I sat, she seemed to have it all, including a privileged, happy life.

We lived in a provincial neighborhood of two-parent families with 2.5 children. The men went to work, the women went to PTA meetings—and sometimes part-time work—and they all gathered with the extended family on Sundays and holidays for dinner. I felt so far from the norm that I wasn't even on the curve. Except for noticing these reminders, however, I had no time to dwell on it. I had other things to do—like survive.

When I received and read the following letter from my carpool neighbor, it had been three or four years since I had seen her. My life was a long way from where it had been, and I had to stop and remember who she was.

Dear Tonja,

I just wanted you to know how much your courage and success have meant to me. I have lived in an abusive relationship for years, terrified of what would happen if I left.

I have watched you struggle, keep your chin up, and, essentially, earn the admiration of everyone who knows you—including me. What you have done with your life is nothing short of amazing.

My husband and I are divorcing, and it is your example that I have clung to in the dark moments. You have given me hope that maybe I too can make it and have a happy life. I cannot thank you enough.

God bless you,
C.M.

Speechless, I tried to absorb what she'd said, what she'd gone through, and what I'd done that would cause her to see something I'd missed. I wasn't aware of being an example to anyone. I was struggling to take care of my responsibilities, to learn from my difficulties, to carve out a present and future that were different from the past. Living a life that was a legacy to others was the furthest thing from my mind.

Over the years, I've thought about the gift her letter was. It's made me pause and look at the legacy I'd received from people I admired that gave me the grit to persevere. Even though I was poor, alone, scared, and far from home, something in me expected myself to make it. My mentors had left an imprint on how I perceived I'd live my life.

Have you thought about your legacy? Whether you realize it or not, while you are shaping a better life day by day, you are having an impact. All the good things you do for yourself ripple out to others. They get the benefits vicariously—and even directly.

Your friends, your children, your family, and your neighbors are all watching you, so take the opportunity to define your own legacy. In this book, chapter by chapter, you've already made the first steps:

The TAO of Divorce

By shifting your old perspective, you and your ex are capable of being kind in one another's presence. Your family, co-workers, and friends all benefit from your different behavior. Your new TAO keeps affirming and inspiring you to look for more insights, reevaluate perceptions, and continue to create a great life.

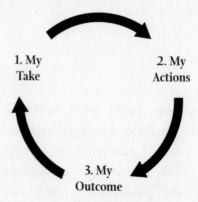

1. My Take

2. My Actions

3. My Outcome

Your positive new Take
creates new Actions,
bringing a new Outcome.

Your legacy is

- Being *appropriate* in all circumstances
- Developing an *attitude of acceptance*
- Maintaining *kindness* in difficult situations
- Extending *friendship* where it's possible

Laying the Groundwork for Transformation

By shifting to a Take that gets you closer to your desired Outcome, you lay the groundwork for transformation. Your Take ripples throughout all your interactions—with your friends, your family, and your former partner and his or her friends and family. Everyone feels comfortable in your presence. When you are civil to your ex, his relatives, and his friends, people feel safe.

Not asking questions about his personal life or sharing inappropriate information about your own keeps the atmosphere clear for conversations that stay calm. When bombs of anger are not exploding and you stay away from unresolved emotional issues, there is no debris to fall on anyone's head.

Your new Take allows people and situations to be the way they are, and you don't expect them to be the way you wish they were. Your focus is on healing, forgiveness, and acceptance.

Why can you do this now? It's easy—because you have a life that feeds you and sustains you and gives you enthusiasm.

Your legacy is

- Keeping your *dignity* at all times
- Maintaining an atmosphere of *calm* and *peace*
- Practicing *kindness* on a daily basis
- Being *civil* to those around you

Taking Stock

Everyone has learned something useful from past relationships, whether it's a new skill or a previously unknown emotional strength. Looking at your breakup through this lens helps you find the tangible good in it.

When you are at a crossroads in life, it's important to stop and take stock. Assessing where you are, what you have to offer, where you want to go, and how to get there helps you focus on your wins rather than your losses. Moving from complaining to finding solutions is a new habit that transforms your entire life.

Listing your various competencies, discovering your gaps and thinking about what you can do about them, and then doing something are how you get from where you are to where you want to be. Taking positive action furthers the trajectory of your life.

Everything you do leaves an imprint on those around you. The way you survive and the steps you take are being watched, imitated (consciously or unconsciously), and left as a memory to others. You now know how to see the challenges in your life as opportunities for growth, not as setbacks. Rather than focusing on what's going wrong or what you don't have, you can be uplifted by the knowledge of all you keep in your heart.

Your legacy is

- Taking stock by doing an assessment that is *realistic*
- *Healing* through positive assessment
- Moving forward in a *courageous* way
- *Enthusiastically* setting out on a course of action

Strengthening Your Boundaries

Learning about boundaries and using what you've learned, you feel protected—from your own injurious behavior and that of others. You'll never be in jeopardy of feeling controlled by situations or people again. You can trust your responses, even in stressful times, because you know not to cross boundaries—yours or others'.

For example, in most relationships that break up, one person wants out more than the other. Your boundaries are your self-preservation. If you feel you are still in love with your ex, even though your ex is dating or married to someone else, keep your boundary close to you, tight (sending no romantic energy in his or her direction), and dignified. As your life continues to improve, the situation just gets easier.

If your ex is the one still in love and you are not, respect your ex's feelings by standing back at a certain distance and not sending messages that will confuse him or her.

If your ex was abusive, verbally or physically, boundaries are essential. Learn to keep a healthy distance. In situations where there are children from the marriage, you may need their visits to be supervised. Your entire family learns how to use boundaries by watching you. Take exquisite care of yourself so you can take care of those who need you.

Liberated from the fear of falling into unhealthy relationships, you welcome the chance to meet new people. Listening to your inner voice, which tells you when a boundary has been crossed, deepens your self-awareness.

Your legacy is

- Gaining *dignity* by respecting others' boundaries
- Refusing to let others trespass over your *boundaries*
- *Respecting* yourself by honoring boundaries
- Using boundaries in all situations, thereby yielding *confidence*

Cleaning House

Your divorce has been the major motivator to clean house. This is the way you have rediscovered your energy. Whenever your enthusiasm starts to flag, you now know what to do: get organized.

Eliminating clutter, fixing things that are broken, organizing closets and drawers, and cleaning house are doors to your new life. Ridding yourself of negative words removes another kind of clutter. Speaking words of hope and honor attracts people who return the same to you.

Emotional litter is "baggage," and cleaning it up comes in the form of asking forgiveness and forgiving others. Wherever you have had harsh words and a lack of understanding or ended a relationship badly, you need to take an action that will clear this hurt. Cleaning up past negativity will smooth the path to better relationships in the future.

For many people, cleaning house can be like a cleansing of the soul. De-cluttering and removing material items that hold bad memories is incredibly liberating. You might consider instituting a yearly ritual of going through every drawer, closet, and room to get rid of what you no longer need or want; the shot of energy from that exercise will make you feel vibrantly alive and ready to move forward in your own, fantastic future.

Your legacy is

- Cleaning up clutter to reduce burdens and bring a sense of *lightness*
- *Maintaining* possessions, thereby eliminating the need to acquire more
- Changing negative words to *positive* ones
- Gaining *freedom* and eliminating baggage by forgiving others

Getting into Alignment

As you pull all the parts of your life together and align your thoughts, words, feelings, and actions, you'll find easy answers to your questions and sense any residual depression lifting.

Identifying your deepest values makes it clear why and how you can get out of alignment—and how to correct it if you do.

To live in alignment is to be honest to the core. You rise to a higher level of integrity with yourself and those around you. Flowing in sync, you are in balance and you have greater discernment than ever before.

Your legacy is

- Leading a *values*-driven life
- Feeling *optimistic* from being in alignment
- Aligning your life and allowing *serenity*
- Building *trust* by living from your values

Building a New Foundation

When you are on a solid footing, you are someone others can count on. Furthermore, *you can count on yourself.* When you have a rock-solid foundation, you can make better choices for your life.

There are certain bricks that help you keep your foundation unshakable. With a network of friends, your finances in order, reserves of health, a strong purpose, and hobbies to get excited about, you are a strong structure.

Regular checklists in each area will help you remain clear about which brick might need more attention at any given time. When you inspect your own foundation for any leaks or cracks, and mend when needed, you will not be clingy or desperate for other people to hold you up.

Your legacy is

- Enjoying physical and emotional *strength*
- Feeling *secure* with foundational bricks under you
- Knowing *stability* while standing on a strong personal foundation
- Experiencing *pride* from building a foundation of integrity

Growing Your New Life

The metaphor of the slow-growing, always-in-flux Zen garden illustrates certain truths that are eternal. Your new life uses this standard as a measure of what needs to be done to flourish.

Looking at the garden, you can see what you need to do: plant yourself where you'll thrive, have a plan for your growth, gather the tools you need, plant what you want to grow, and keep your soil enriched.

Gardening teaches patience, hard work, consistency, realism, the importance of keeping agreements, and forgiveness. The unfinished nature of the Zen garden mirrors your own new life. Whether your gardening thumb is green or not, caring for another living thing can be a great way to soothe your emotions and create a space of serenity—whether it's a potted plant on your apartment's windowsill or a lush garden behind your home. Tending your garden is a way to remind yourself of the care required for every living thing—especially you!

Your legacy is

- Knowing the concept of *planning* through gardening
- Maintaining *discipline* to achieve success
- Showing *fortitude* in order to sustain growth
- Planting, tending, feeding, and weeding for *gorgeous results*

Getting What You Want

You are now in a higher zone of expectation and performance. Because you've discovered the practical and mysterious use of energy, you have learned the art of giving yourself what you want.

Choosing a goal, putting your focus on it, visualizing it, feeling what it would be like to have it, taking action, believing it will happen, and then letting it go all add up to a process you can use over and over. As you manifest what you want, others notice and feel hope. As you succeed, you teach. It's like a stone thrown into a pond; the ripple effect moves far beyond you, touching people you might never meet. And this technique is not something magical or unique; it's something we can all do.

Your legacy is

- Feeling *satisfaction* from creating what you want
- Focusing on personal goals for heightened *clarity*
- *Achieving* consistent results
- Knowing how to create a better life, which gives you *confidence*

Thriving with Creativity

Creativity helps you not only survive but also thrive. This resource is often dormant—an unused asset that can be activated at any time. Now is your moment to seize the power that lies within.

Using your creativity helps you reinvent yourself. Whenever you feel confused about your future, you turn to your creative methods for discovering where you want to be, what you want to do, and how you want to do it. Sourcing your creativity for new answers brings the solutions that make your life authentic, viable, and fulfilled.

When your own creativity goes unacknowledged, you will likely feel out of step with the rest of the world, or feel that what seemed to be easy for others is a challenge for you. Even getting back to your so-called normal life can be overwhelming. Yet by understanding the blessings and challenges of creativity, you can learn to accept the way you are instead of fighting it.

Your legacy is

- Being a true *original* by accessing your creativity
- Creating a life of *authenticity*
- Solving challenges creatively, which develops *fearlessness*
- Living creatively to feed and sustain *joy*

Considering New Relationships

Arriving at this point in your growth, you have learned enough to know you are ready to take full responsibility for the quality of your relationships. With new criteria for friendship, you recognize where you need boundaries. With your deeper awareness of self, you have an expanded capacity for communication. There is now a surge of positive energy around all components of your life, and you look for relationships that are mutually beneficial.

You may now be ready to expand your social life to include dating. When you do, you have a steady perception of your personal values and how to be in alignment. This is how you attract someone who shares similar standards.

With this new assessment of who you are, and holding yourself to a new level of integrity, you set out with some dating tools that are appropriate for your situation. You are empowered. The wisdom you've gained from the passage of divorce now supports a new social life that is yours to design and enjoy.

Armed with the lessons you've learned, developing a new social life without always having a significant other at your side can be thrilling and liberating. Finally, you will be able to trust your choices and decisions; when you know who you are deep inside, you will clearly see what is good for you and what isn't. Until then, you may not even realize that you're looking for someone (or something) to fill a need. Having this knowledge shifts the whole way you now approach dating.

Your legacy is

- Planning a rich and varied social life full of *excitement*
- Respecting personal *values*
- Feeling *empowered* by exercising boundaries in relationships
- Developing better, more *rewarding* social skills

Knowing that you will be leaving a legacy can motivate you to do something difficult—like starting a new life—in a way that honors all that you are and all that you have the potential to become. Your breakup or divorce was the catalyst, and by doing the work throughout these chapters, you've learned the tools and gained the skills that will shape your legacy. You are now ready to thrive in the life you have always wanted.

Afterword: Continuing the Journey

The end of your relationship may have brought pain, regret, and a deep sense of loss. My hope is that, with the help of this book, you have crossed over into a place of strength, wisdom, and delicious excitement for what your future holds. I also hope that you have developed a new TAO that has enhanced your opportunities, brought clarity to your challenges, and given you enthusiasm to continue your journey.

- Transformation has come from forgiveness and allowing.
- Taking stock has helped you focus on your strengths.
- You feel safe because you have boundaries in place.
- De-cluttering has left you with renewed energy.
- Your Actions are aligned with your values.
- You are clear about strengthening your bricks for your foundation.
- Your new life is growing in harmony, like a Zen garden.
- You now have the tools to attract what you want.
- The energy of creativity assists you in reinventing yourself.
- Your new relationships are positive experiences, feeding your growth.

- You recognize that all your accomplishments and wins shine a light for others.

Take a breath, sit back, and think about your new TAO. It may look something like this:

My Take: I am a courageous, bright, and beautiful light in the world.

My Actions: I continue to learn, grow, and appreciate everything I am.

My Outcome: I have an exquisite life.

You deserve this TAO. The journey is just beginning, so let your new TAO show you the way and live in the moment.